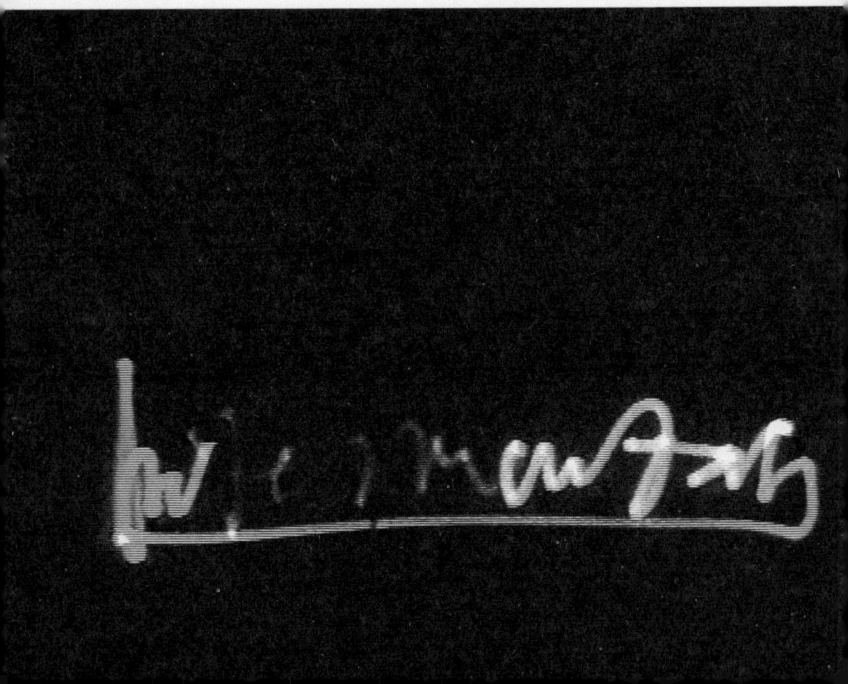

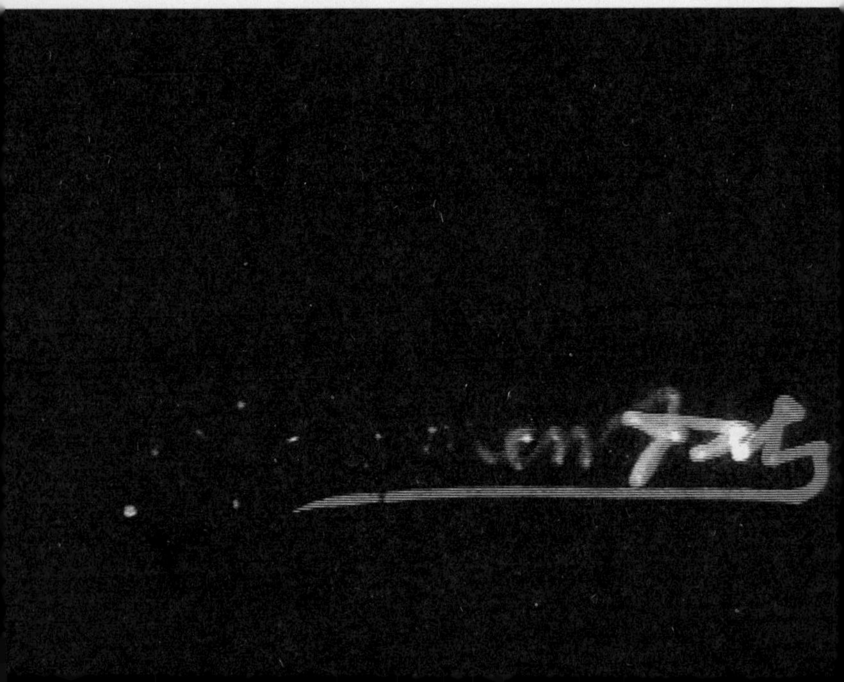

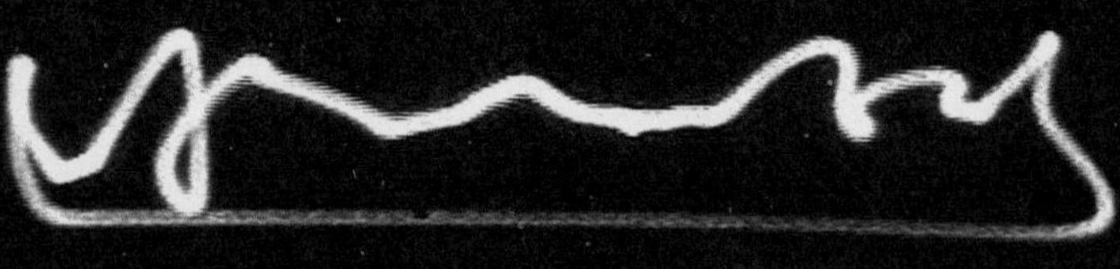

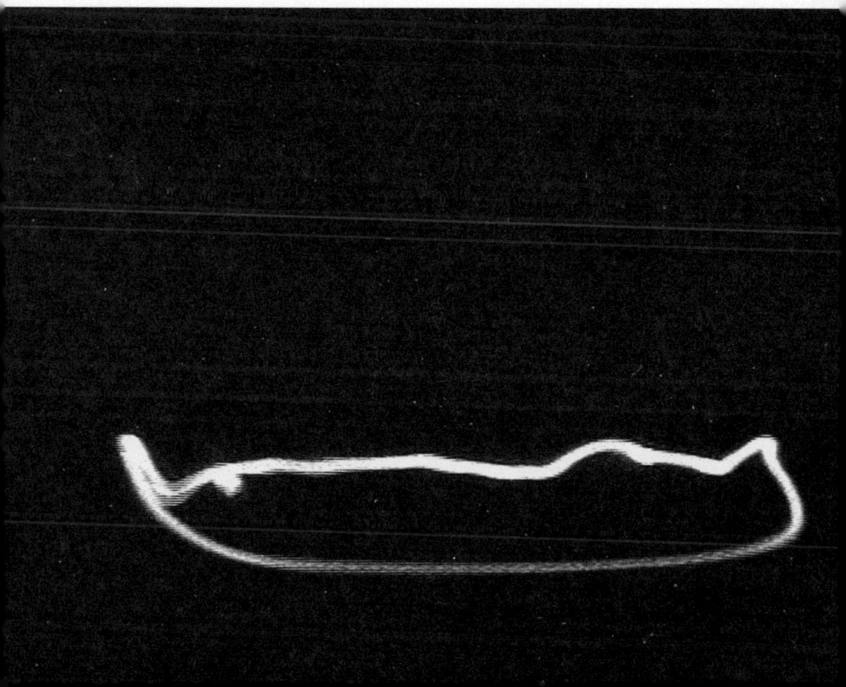

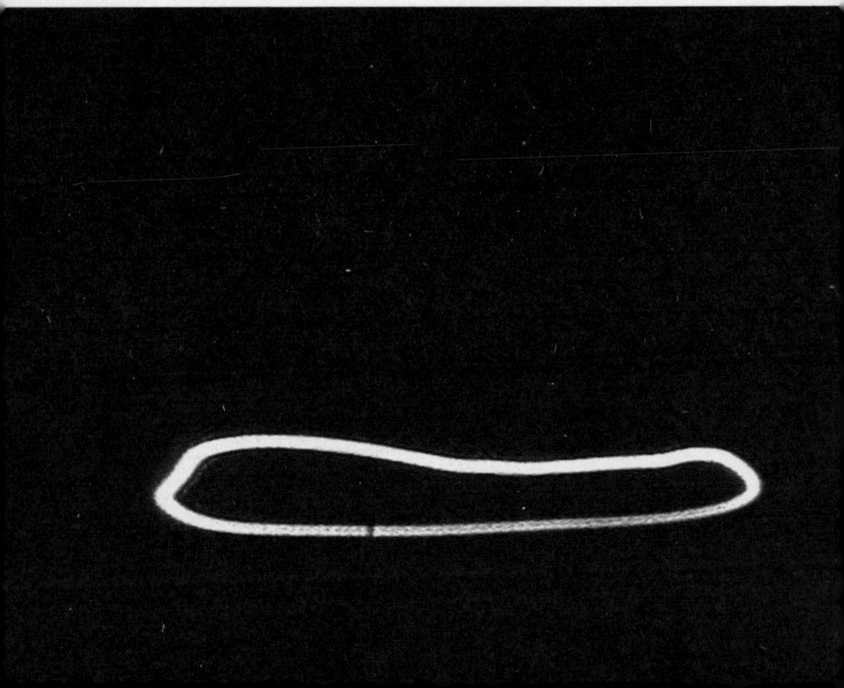

A Detour Around Infermental

George Clark
Dan Kidner
James Richards

Focal Point Gallery

Foreword

In 2009 Focal Point Gallery invited George Clark and Dan Kidner to organise an exhibition based on *Infermental*, Gábor and Vera Bódy's video publication that was produced in Hungary between 1980 and 1990. The reason for commissioning this project twenty years after the original journal's end was due to the curators' obvious enthusiasm for the critical potential of *Infermental*'s relaxed aesthetic model, its varied formats, as well as for its model of distribution, and what this might mean to a younger generation of artist filmmakers. Perhaps in an age when professionalism increasingly dominates the field of contemporary artists' moving image in the UK, or high production values progressively and unquestioningly purport to represent good practice, *Infermental* characterises a rigorously agile and informal alternative, and acts as a fluid and collaborative historical model for us to learn from.

For the exhibition in Southend-on-Sea, which took place between July and September 2010, Clark and Kidner unearthed three of the eleven issues of the publication from the archive and screened them in their entirety to an audience who would have almost certainly needed to be in attendance for the full seven-week duration of the exhibition to witness the large volume of work it contained.

With the addition of James Richards' exhibition design, which comprised viewing platforms mirroring minimal sculpture, and reproductions of *Infermental* posters, this marathon display fulfilled its intention to activate a neat curatorial twist on the subjective representation of historical material, in one sense as a contemporary artwork in its own right. In turn, this book, entitled *A Detour Around Infermental*, intends to throw into question historical interpretation through the additional discursive elements provided by Richards and the artist and designer Will Holder. The interviews contained within it act as an enquiry into the original manifestation of *Infermental* and a reflective questioning of the process of its participants' subsequent cumulative investigations.

As the first major analysis of *Infermental* anywhere in the world, a sense of responsibility was needed when approaching this project, but not one that ran against the experimental nature of the original work. As a developing organisation, we are very proud of the resulting exhibition and publication that Clark, Kidner and Richards have produced, and thrilled to have been able to host and facilitate such an important piece of research. It's fair to say that this impulse for new knowledge connects clearly with the gallery's wider aim to provide a vibrant and varied programme not only for the connecting audiences of Southend-on-Sea and a related international context, but also with our intention to offer a regular slot each year to a young curator (or in this case, a collaborative curatorial enterprise) to engage meticulously with a specific interest in contemporary film and video.

I would like to thank all of the people involved with the exhibition 'Infermental' and *A Detour Around Infermental*, including Vera Baksa-Soós for her help with realising the project, George Clark, Dan Kidner, James Richards for their enthusiasm throughout the planning of the exhibition and the production of this publication, Will Holder for designing a wonderful exhibition poster, Jo Baxendale, Georgia Ward and Andrea Stark at Arts Council England for their ongoing support with the development of Focal Point Gallery and its programme, Simon May and his staff at Southend-on-Sea Central Library, Simon Leftley, Nick Harris and Rosemary Pennington at Southend-on-Sea Borough Council for their constant encouragement and assistance, the team at Focal Point Gallery for their unbound energy and James Langdon for his imaginative and beautiful book design.

Andrew Hunt
Director, Focal Point Gallery

Introduction

The conversations in this book were recorded in February and April 2011. They followed the exhibition, 'Infermental', which took place from 19 July to 4 September 2010 at Focal Point Gallery. The show, curated by George Clark and Dan Kidner, with James Richards, surveyed *Infermental*, the 'first international magazine on videocassettes', which was initiated in 1980 by Gábor and Vera Bódy. A specially built screening room and three viewing platforms hosted three of the eleven issues of the 'magazine' that were produced between 1980 and 1991.

Gábor Bódy's idea was to build an 'Encyclopaedia of Recorded Imagery'. The first issues were realised with boundless energy and a visionary zeal; though Bódy, the project's figurehead, died in 1985, *Infermental* continued for another six years. The first issue was produced whilst Bódy was on a DAAD residency in Berlin, and each subsequent issue was put together in a different city. Beginning in Europe, and with a distinct focus on connecting video and media artists in the east and the west, *Infermental* became a project with global reach when later editions were produced in North America and Japan. Each edition featured between thirty and one-hundred artists contributing complete films, excerpts, trailers, interviews, filmed performances and fragments, and was assembled by a different editorial team, normally consisting of two former contributors, and one supervisor.

Over the course of the project's life, a diverse range of influential figures contributed to the magazine including Margaret Ahwesh, Tony Conrad, Gary Hill, Joan Jonas, Jon Jost, Marcel Odenbach, Amos Poe, Steina Vasulka and Lawrence Weiner. But what makes it such a fascinating and enduring project were the less familiar names, the editorial rationale, the innovative distribution strategy and presentation. Enabled by the newly accessible technology of U-matic video, *Infermental* brought together a range of formats including 8mm, 16mm and 35mm, as well as video. The editions were sold or hired to institutions with specific instructions for their presentation: the tapes were to be played one after the other for the full duration of the issue. Given the status of video at this time, and broad lack of support from galleries and film festivals, *Infermental* attempted to find a new way to present and circulate work amongst artists and institutions around the world.

Rather than present the full archive, the exhibition at Focal Point Gallery focused on just three issues that at once represent the range and ambition of the project, but also narrate the project's development from a European network to a global community of experimental filmmakers and new media artists. Issue one appeared in 1982 and explicitly made the relationship between east and west its overarching theme. There are also six subthemes under which the works were grouped. The first, 'The Mirror as Motif', includes several artists who would go on to be involved in the project as it evolved over the years: Gusztáv Hámos, Astrid Heibach and Rotraut Pape. The fourth issue was edited by the French artists group Frigo, and marks a shift in the editorial policy, drawing on the group's multi-disciplinary activities, collective organisation and experience in pirate radio. Authorship is problematised as amateur footage, highly authored artists' films, ethnographic documents, video performances and music videos are seamlessly edited together. Issue eight, produced in Tokyo and edited by Keiko Sei and Alfred Birnbaum, was the final edition included in the exhibition. With the title 'In the Afterglow of TV-land' it signalled the limit of the project's global ambitions and drew together a diverse range of practitioners in a constant flow of information that resembled an alternative TV broadcast. In addition to these three issues, one monitor showed *Cross-Cultural Television* (1987) by Hank Bull and Antonio Muntadas, a video specially commissioned to conclude *Infermental 6* (1987), the title of which was 'The New World Edition'.

Part one of the conversation took place between the exhibition's curators George Clark and Dan Kidner and was moderated by Will Holder, who designed the programme notes and the exhibition's poster.

Part two took place between Clark, Kidner and James Richards, who collaborated with the curators on the concept and design of the exhibition.

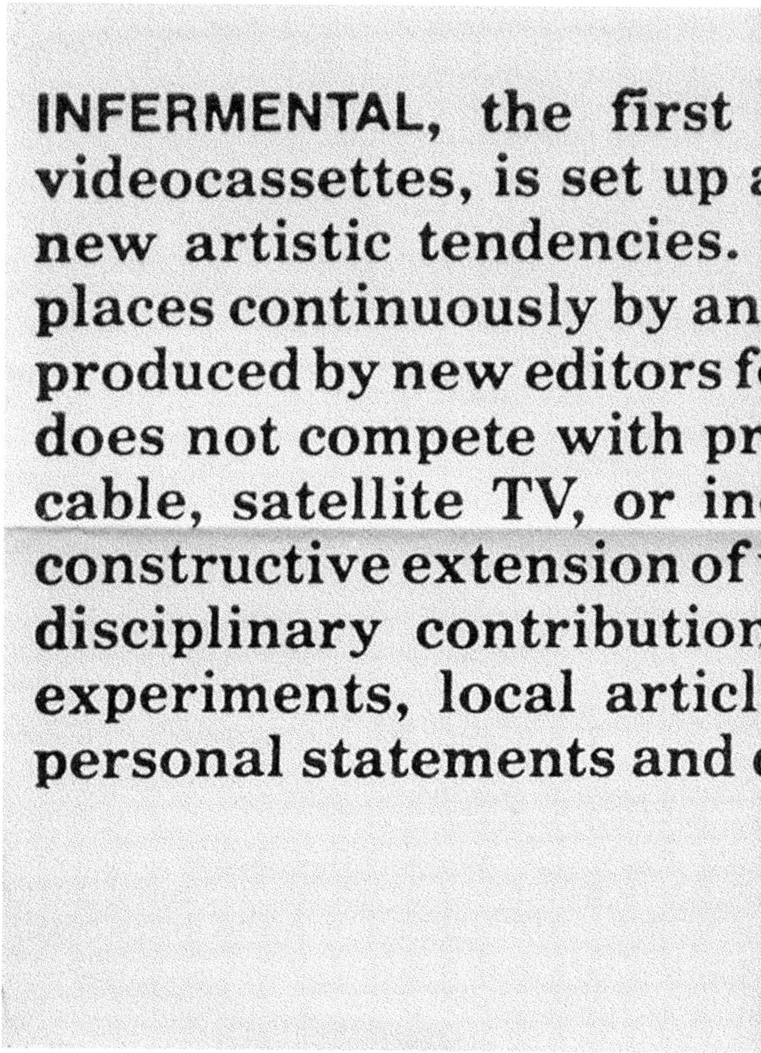

INFERMENTAL, the first
videocassettes, is set up
new artistic tendencies.
places continuously by an
produced by new editors
does not compete with pr
cable, satellite TV, or in
constructive extension of
disciplinary contribution
experiments, local articl
personal statements and

Poster with description of *Infermental* c.1983,
courtesy ZKM | Center for Art and Media, Karlsruhe.

ernational magazine on
a type of encyclopedia for
ERMENTAL moves to new
dependent network, and is
ach edition. INFERMENTAL
ent media systems such as
endent networks. It is a
eo media presenting inter-
such as film clips, video
music video, interviews,
umentations.

A Detour Around Infermental

Part I
4 February 2011

Dan Kidner
George Clark
Will Holder

Dan Kidner — It would be good to start by looking at the origins of *Infermental*, the self-styled 'magazine on video cassettes' [1] initiated by husband and wife Gábor and Vera Bódy [2] in 1980. Then we could move on to look at a number of issues around exhibiting film and video archives in the gallery space. George, maybe you could start by talking a little about Gábor Bódy and his work prior to setting up *Infermental*.

George Clark — The origins of *Infermental* are generally understood to be a number of discussions that took place during Gábor Bódy's involvement with experimental film in the late 1970s. He had formed the experimental film group K/3 [3] at the Béla Balázs Studio,[4] Budapest, in 1976. This was a workshop that aimed to explore the possibilities of film, its relationship to language as well as to different, possible modes of experimental practice. Bódy started to discuss setting up a network that would link filmmakers, initially

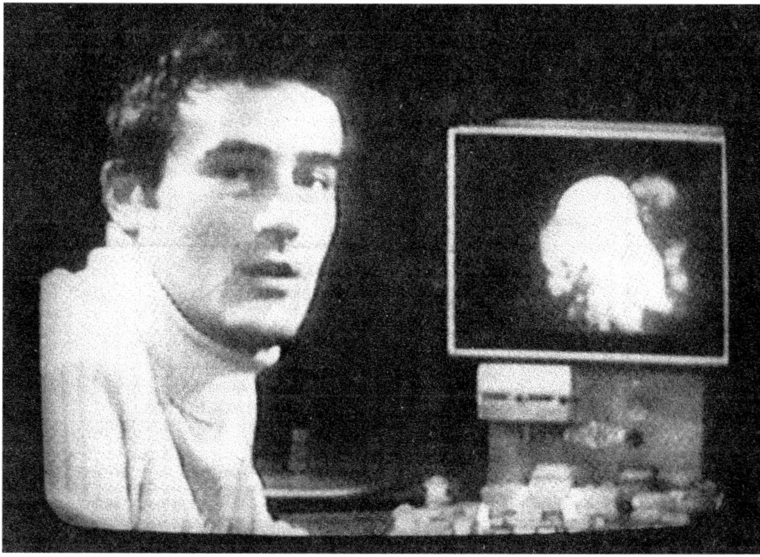

Frame enlargement from *Film School*, 16mm, black and white, dir. Gabór Bódy, Magyar Televízió, 1976, from *Bódy Gabór 1946–1985, A Presentation of His Work*, eds. László Beke, Miklós Peternák (1987, Budapest: Mucsarnok), p. 108.

1
In documents from 1981/1982 relating to the first issue of *Infermental*, the project is described as, 'The international video cassette periodical with new experiments for ear and eye.' By the time of *Infermental 4* in 1985, this definition had been changed to: 'The first international magazine on videocassettes.'

2
Gábor Bódy (Budapest, Hungary, 1946 to 1985) and Veruschka 'Vera' Baksa-Soós (Budapest, Hungary, b.1952) married in December 1980.

3
The experimental film group K/3 was founded in 1976. Previous to this, in 1973, Bódy had organised the 'Film Language Series' at the Béla Balázs Studio, which was the first experimental film project at the studio and involved artists, musicians and writers as well as filmmakers. See László Beke, Miklós Peternák (eds.), *Bódy Gabór 1946–1985. A Presentation of His Work* (1987, Budapest: Mucsarnok).

4
The Béla Balázs Studio was unique in Eastern Europe. It was started as a film club in 1959, and in 1961 became a film studio that worked both within and outside of the strict structure of state film production. Over the course of more than fifty years it produced and distributed more than five-hundred films in all genres, from shorts, through to documentary and major feature films, as well as experimental film and video. As well as Bódy, several stars of Hungarian cinema started their careers there including Béla Tarr, Sándor Sára and János Xantus. The studio also provided space for practitioners from other fields including writers, musicians, visual artists and sociologists. See www.bbsarchiv.hu

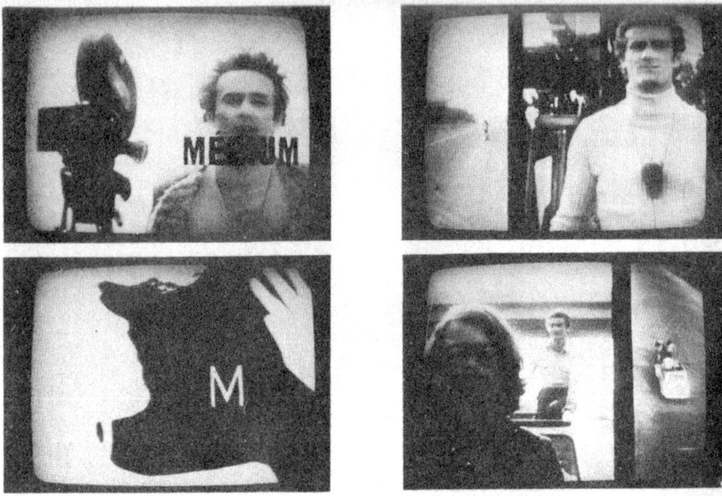

Four frame enlargements from *Film School*, 16mm, black and white, dir. Gabór Bódy, Magyar Televízió, 1976, from *Bódy Gabór 1946–1985, A Presentation of His Work*, eds. László Beke, Miklós Peternák (1987, Budapest: Mucsarnok), p. 111.

5
The name 'Infermental' is a portmanteau, though the exact words that were used vary according to different sources. A call for submissions to the first issue made in October 1981 stated that *Infermental* is 'a combination of the words "international", "fermentum" and "experimental", whilst the www.infermental.de website states that the final word is derived from "mental".' The meaning of 'fermentum' is disputed amongst contributors to the project. Some claim that it merely represents 'ferment' which, deriving from the Latin word fermentum, also has an explicitly religious meaning. *The Concise Oxford Dictionary of the Christian Church* (2000) includes the definition: 'In Rome (5th cent.), the fragments of the Bread of the Eucharist sent on Sundays from the Papal Mass to presbyters in the parish churches to typify the unity of the faithful in Christ.' This allusion is plausible, given Bódy's use of overt Catholic imagery in his work at this time.

6
The proposed series, *Filmiskola*, which would have included twenty educational films, was to be produced for Magyar Televízió (the Hungarian national public service television company). Only three episodes were completed in 1976. The scripts and plans for the series were published in Hungary in 1998 by Palatinus Kiadó as Filmiskola. See László Beke, Miklós Peternák (eds.), *Bódy Gabór 1946–1985. A Presentation of His Work* (1987, Budapest: Mucsarnok).

within Eastern Europe, but with the ambition to go further than that. The first conversations took place at a festival in Poland in the autumn of 1980 — this is where the name 'Infermental' was established.[5] At that time it was proposed that *Infermental* would take the form of an encyclopaedia of new media practice. This was in 1980 …

Will Holder — An encyclopaedia … That's what they called it or that's what you call it?

George Clark — That's what they called it. This original group of filmmakers all put their name to the proposal for an encyclopaedia project that they wanted to see realised. This definition was very much related to Bódy's interest in semiotics: he had already made a series of films on this subject — a pedagogical project called *Film School* (1976), which took the form of a series of filmed lectures augmented with different demonstrations of experimental techniques.[6]

The proposal that was signed by the Polish and Hungarian filmmakers in 1980 also laid the groundwork for how this international network was going to be formalised. But it wasn't until Gábor Bódy was in Berlin, on a DAAD residency, in the early 1980s that he found a way to actually realise this project, though by that time it was at a distance from the Polish filmmakers with whom it had initially been discussed. So *Infermental* was formalised through

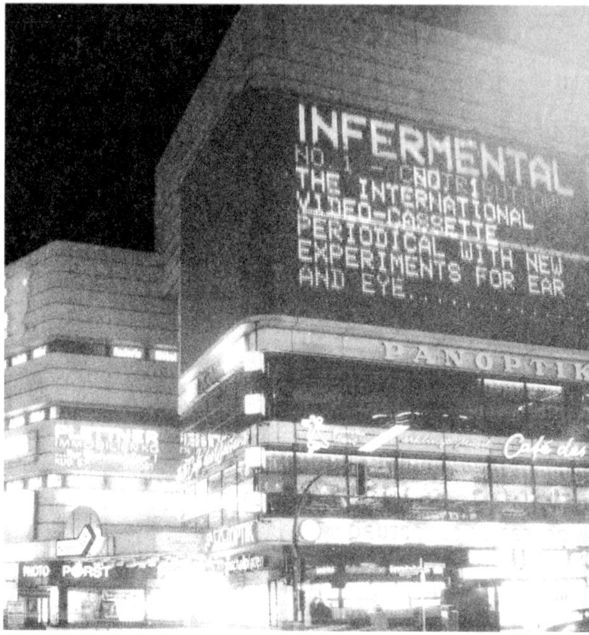

Infermental launch, West Berlin, 1982. Photo by Zoltan Jancsu, © Vera Baksa-Soós, courtesy ZKM | Center for Art and Media, Karlsruhe.

7
'Gusztáv Hámos (b.1955, Budapest, Hungary) lives and works in Berlin. His first film and photo works date back to 1972–8. In 1979 he emigrated to West Berlin. In 1980 he began his studies at the Deutschen Film- und Fernsehakademie, Berlin [...] Since 1980 he works with video on an artistic level, realises TV productions and installations.' From http://archive.transmediale.de/site07/persons+M5aa3077f613.html

8
As part of the Berlin International Film Festival, the Internationales Forum des Jungen Films was founded in 1971 by Ulrich Gregor and Manfred Salzgeber.

9
'Astrid Heibach (b.1949, Düsseldorf, Germany) studied film at the Kunstakademie in Düsseldorf. In 1992 she received the German video art award. She edited the first edition of the video magazine *Infermental* with Gábor Bódy, who initiated this project in 1980. Heibach lives and works in Cologne.' From http://archive.transmediale.de/site07/persons+M5e0f035309d.html

10
Amerikai Anzix (American Torso, Hungary, 1975) and *Nárcisz és Psyché* (Narcissus and Psyche, Hungary, 1980).

— and funded by — Bódy's DAAD grant. The production of the first issue was supported technically by the Deutschen Film- und Fernsehakademie, Berlin (DFFB), which was facilitated by Gusztáv Hámos,[7] a Hungarian-born video artist who was studying there at the time. So that's the first time that *Infermental*, which before was this speculative idea, was defined and put into practice.

The other crucial institution was the International Forum of New Cinema[8] at the Berlin International Film Festival: Ulrich Gregor, the Forum's Director, had supported Bódy's film work, and made a commitment to show *Infermental 1*, which was first screened at the Berlinale in February 1982.

Dan Kidner When assembling the first issue, Bódy and Astrid Heibach[9] put out a call for submissions. This was basically sent to Bódy's existing network, which at that point was still quite small, and included a lot of the filmmakers he had met in Berlin and at festivals. This meant that virtually everything that was submitted made the edition.

But even before developing the ideas that would form the *Infermental* project, Bódy was a fairly established experimental filmmaker in Hungary, working out of the Béla Balázs Studio. He had already directed two well-received feature films that were quite widely shown at international film festivals.[10] By this point he had already been experimenting with video for some years.

George Clark — The Béla Balázs Studio was a state-funded structure that would allow filmmakers to make their first short film, prior to becoming part of the Hungarian film industry. The real change came in 1969, when the studio produced its first feature film: it was by a director called Deszö Magyar and was called *Agitátorok* (Agitators); Bódy co-wrote the script and also appeared in the film.[11] That was really the shift, as the studio then started to explore how it could provide a parallel context in which filmmakers could make features outside of the official state-run film industry. The K/3 group would bring in other practitioners, who weren't necessarily involved in filmmaking, with whom to collaborate. So the idea was to work with painters and musicians, and to have this film studio that wasn't so geared towards a certain type of industrial production.

Will Holder — But did they see themselves as a school in that sense?

George Clark — Bódy definitely had this pedagogical intent. I think in some ways K/3 was his attempt to create a link between the institutional framework of the Béla Balázs Studio and the avant-garde movements within Hungary … As an organiser and a spokesman, Bódy was a very powerful presence.

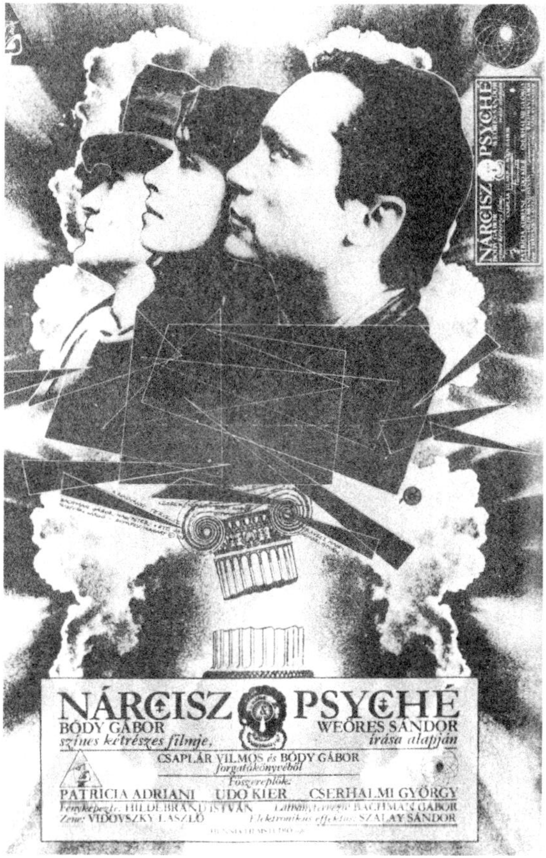

Nárcisz és Psyché (*Narcissus and Psyche*), theatrical film poster, c.1980, from *Bódy Gabór 1946–1985, A Presentation of His Work*, eds. László Beke, Miklós Peternák (1987, Budapest: Mucsarnok).

11
Agitátorok (Agitators, 1969) 82 minutes, 35mm film, based on the novel *Optimisták* (The Optimists, 1953) by Ervin Sinkó. The film was banned and it was not shown publically in Hungary until 1986. Recalling his involvement, in 1979 Bódy stated: 'I regard my participation in Agitators as my first proper cinematic work. This was directed by Dezso Magyar, but I also took part in writing the scenario and in the direction.' From László Beke, Miklós Peternák (eds.), *Bódy Gabór 1946–1985. A Presentation of His Work* (1987, Budapest: Mucsarnok), p.67.

Dan Kidner Early on he had conceived *Infermental* as a school. He called it a 'non-geographical Bauhaus', and right from the start the function of it was to unite practitioners from the east and west. That was the utopian dream if you like: that *Infermental* should cross these boundaries. Whether Bódy actually saw the future in the way that it played out is difficult to say, but that's something we'll come back to.

Will Holder It seems to also tie in with a certain form of conceptualism that was being produced in the Eastern Bloc at the time, one that was developed according to its own prescription and its own rules. It made quite a split from Western-dominated forms …

Dan Kidner Well, in terms of an Anglo-American idea of conceptual art, I think what's happening here is something quite different. In the early stages of *Infermental*, and especially given Bódy's connection to Berlin, there is certainly a very different idea about crossing disciplines it's actually a non-conceptual idea about mixing up disciplines. There's a much more fluid idea of what it means to have a multimedia practice, which is not 'conceptual' in the way that you would understand the practices that were coming from the UK or US tradition, both of which were tied to different notions of medium-specificity.

The broader context of Berlin in the early 1980s is really important here, because that's the scene that many of the artists contributing to *Infermental* were emerging from. At that time a lot of new music was coming out of the city: the punk and post-punk scenes there had taken a particularly industrial and apocalyptic turn, and a lot of this was reflected in the videos that made it into those first few issues. Music was key to the project in general. Many of the videos and films even take the form of quasi-music videos — and some actually are early music videos.[12]

George Clark From the beginning, *Infermental* was never going to be an attempt to create an ideal space for work; it was always going to be an anthology, or a sampling of these different practices.

Will Holder So it was less about production and more about distribution?

Dan Kidner Yes, or more about trying to force, or facilitate, a dialogue between different types of practice.

George Clark In that way, even the conceptual works that are contained within it are sampled.

Dan Kidner But I don't think Bódy and the editors were critical or reflective in that sense; decisions about the structure of the project were made much more pragmatically. Also the project lay, in many ways, outside of the art world — or its ambitions lay outside the narrow concerns of a small group of

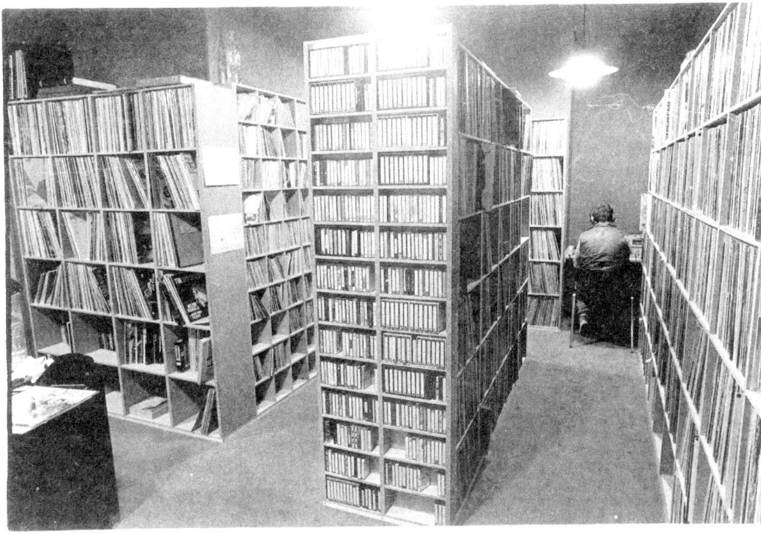

Radio Bellevue was the radio station created by members of Frigo and ran between 1981 and 1989 in Lyon, photo courtesy Gérard Couty.

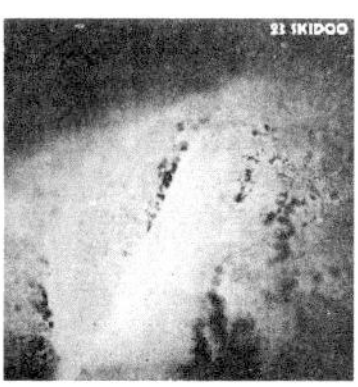

Skidoo 23, *Coup*, released by Illuminated, UK, 1984.

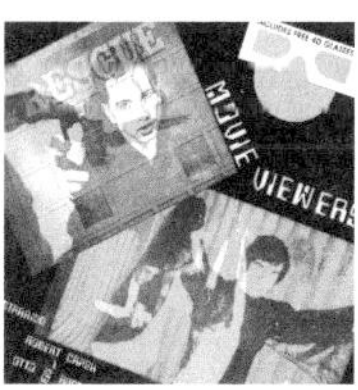

Rescue 1 (Otto Von Ruggins, Robert Crash), *Movie Viewers*, released by MLP, USA, 1981.

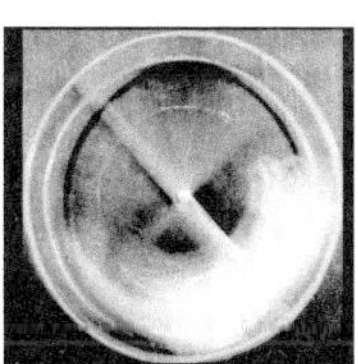

Yello, *Bostich*, released by Do It Records, UK, 1981.

12
Such as *Movie Viewers for Rescue 1* (Otto Von Ruggins and Robert Crash) in *Infermental 1*, Skidoo 23's video *Coup*, Ute Meta Bauer's video with the performance group Paris Ruft and Laibach Kunst's *The Debate over Man* in *Infermental 4*, and various videos for Yello (Boris Blank, Boris / Meier, Dieter u.a.) such as *The Evening's Young* in *Infermental 2*, *Bostich* in *Infermental 4* and *Pinball Cha Cha* in *Infermental 5* among others.

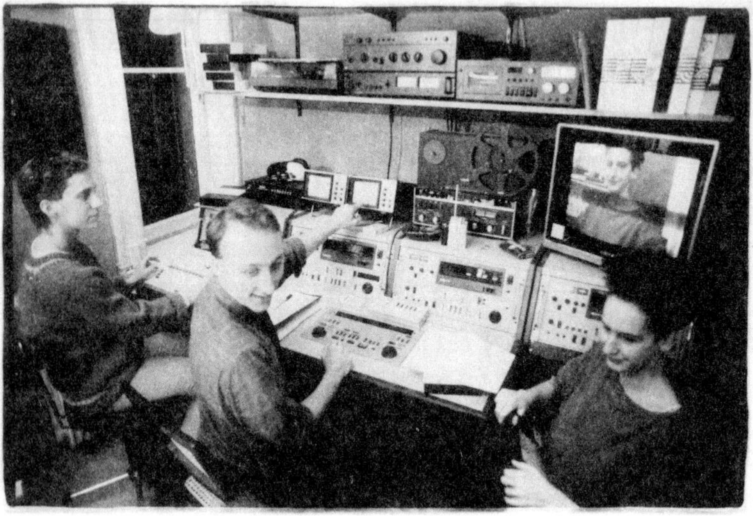

Oliver Hirschbiegel, Rotraut Pape and Vera Bódy in the editing suit preparing *Infermental II* in 1982. Photo courtesy Gérard Couty.

13

In this instance the new media was videotape, and in particular the Sony U-matic tape. Originally introduced in 1971, this was among the first tape formats to contain the videotape inside a cassette as opposed to open reels. In the early 1980s, high-band or Broadcast Video U-matic was launched, which had higher resolution and a greatly improved colour recording system. This internationally standard format made it possible to easily transfer a range of different formats onto one continuous tape, which could then be distributed easily and widely shown.

Vera Bódy described the situation of video production in Hungary at this time in her article 'Magyar Video', published in *Mediamatic Magazine* Vol. 1 #4, 1987: 'Unesco set up a Sony high-band studio in the Seventies at the Országos Oktatási Központ (National Institute for Educational Issues) in Veszprém for the production of audiovisual educational material for Hungarian schools. After five years, the studio was also made available for commercial use so that the production of *Infermental 3* in Veszprém (which was compiled by the Béla Balázs Studio) was in fact made at the going rates for rental. The first official place where video art is produced is the Béla Balázs Studio in Budapest. Here, people are also admitted who are neither students nor employees and have small storyboards and sketches for the production of a video. But only simple low-band equipment is available: a few U-matic, VHS and Beta cameras and a low-band editing suite with a high-band player.'

artists operating across North America and Western Europe at the end of the 1960s.

George Clark: Bódy was much more into semantics than he was into art, so he was interested in the potential of the language of film and video. There was a neutrality in the way that *Infermental* was pitched — it wasn't driven by a desire to profile a new type of art or a specific discourse around contemporary art. They were interested in the potential of new technology to bring together different types of work.[13] And in some ways there was also an element of practical exchange: filmmakers could see how other filmmakers were using these technologies, and then they were able to make other types of work.

Dan Kidner: *Infermental* was explicitly conceived as a 'magazine on video cassettes', so it was not a mobile film festival, and it was not an anthology — it was a magazine. The sampling metaphor that George used before is apt. Editorially, the way the editions were put together resembled the process of assembling an issue of a magazine. The editors — and there was usually a team of two new editors for each issue — collated all the material that they felt best captured that particular moment, or that year. This material was then edited together, often with little regard for the films or videos as individual works; each edition was very much a snapshot of current practice, rather than a fixed programme. The material was also divided between five and seven categories or themes. In terms of current exhibition practice this is very interesting, because today the editors would probably be called curators.

George Clark *Infermental* was very different to something like *Aspen*, the multimedia magazine that was published by Phyllis Johnson between 1965 and 1971. *Aspen* was conceived as an exhibition that you could receive through the mail, containing separate sets of works assembled by a singular editor or designer.[14]

Will Holder But a lot of these projects also problematised the idea of distribution: the distribution of the work of art, or the distribution of production, or the production of distribution.

Dan Kidner As an object itself, *Aspen* was a discrete entity, and the contributions were often specific artworks that were designed to function, critically, within that system of distribution. I don't think that Bódy, or anyone working on the project, had an institutionally critical concept for *Infermental* in that way — it was much more utopian. For him it was about building a network and a community through what he conceived as a 'magazine'. So what you got from watching an edition of *Infermental* was a flavour of what was going on, rather than a series of tightly conceived conceptual artworks — it was open to a cultural moment. I think that's what Bódy was

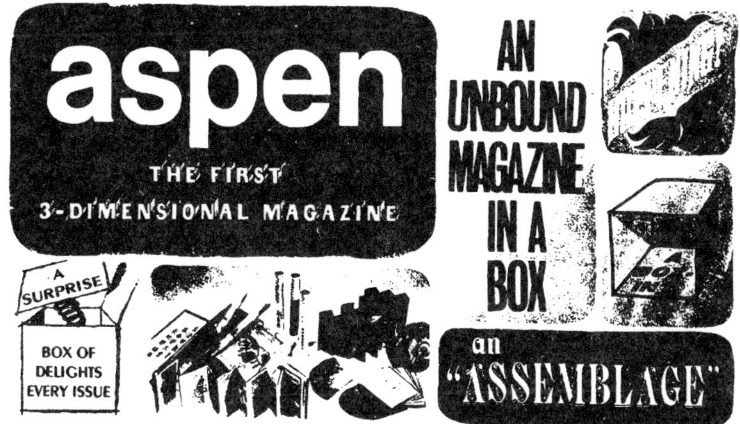

ASPEN IS the first truly new idea in publishing since paperbacks. It is pioneering a revolutionary magazine format: a slender, sturdy 3-dimensional box filled to all of its dimensions with a wealth of reading and hearing and touching and moving and thinking matter.

Each article is a separate booklet, complete in itself. Each takes whatever size and shape and format its content dictates. It makes for exciting, imaginative uses of color and design and materials and ideas.

Why? Why not? Must a magazine always be just a bunch of pages stapled together—limited forever by the restrictions of its binding and by century-old ideas about periodical publishing? We couldn't see any reason why it must.

You'll find almost anything in an ASPEN box. We put each issue of our magazine entirely in the creative hands of a *different* graphic artist-designer . . . so the results are bound to be unpredictable and utterly unique in magazine history—even our own history!

Andy Warhol, for instance, put our Pop/Underground issue in a Fab box. Then filled it with the first "underground movie flip book," a postcard kit of famous pop and op paintings, a rock and roll "press kit," an underground newspaper called "The Plastic Exploding Inevitable."

Our Marshall McLuhan issue unfurled a 32-page press proof from his latest book, a psychedelic wall poster, excerpts from a diary of John Cage, a record of electronic music (every ASPEN box contains at least one LP recording). And the current issue on Far Eastern Thought, designed by Nori Sinoto, comes complete with rolled scrolls, miniature screens and fans, poem cards, even a dragon kite—all scented with incense.

You don't simply read ASPEN . . . you hear it, hang it, feel it, fly it, sniff it, play with it. But ASPEN is not just a conversation piece for artists. It is intended to delight the mind as well as the eye. Its content is as original and unexpected and rewarding as its format.

ASPEN's editorial scope: all the ideas that enhance life, that make it meaningful and give it style and verve. Its coverage: everything that can be described as the civilized pleasures of living—the adventurous in architecture, art, music (always with a record), dance, avant-garde theater and underground movies, nature and conservation, gourmet dining, iconoclastic people . . . and much, much more.

Why do we call it ASPEN? That cultural spa of the Rockies seemed to us a citadel of the exuberant, individualistic life we want our magazine to reflect. We've used it as a symbol, a point of departure for our free wheeling, eclectic approach to modern living (much as The New Yorker uses New York).

Is ASPEN The Magazine in a Box for you? We have a tempting subscription rate to help you find out. As you would expect, a magazine like ASPEN isn't cheap. Three dimensions naturally cost more to produce than two. ASPEN is published four times a year at $4 per issue. But try it on our money-saving subscription offer—and pay just $10.95 for one year (4 issues).

Pay later if you prefer. But if you send payment with your order, saving us bookkeeping and billing costs, we'll reward you with a free gift: a small surprise that will be a delightful preview of ASPEN itself. You risk nothing, of course. Anytime you decide ASPEN is not for you, you may cancel your subscription and pay only for the issues mailed.

Mail the coupon today and your subscription will begin with the inscrutable Far East issue.

aspen

Magazine P.O. Box [illegible] New York, N.Y. 10014

☐ ASPEN sounds like it's for me. Start my subscription with the current issue and send me one year (4 issues) for just $10.95—a saving of $5.05 over the regular single copy cost of $16.

☐ I'm so sure ASPEN is for me. I want to take advantage of your subscription rate for two years. Send me 8 issues for $19.95

☐ I'm enclosing payment. Send me a free surprise.

☐ I prefer to pay later. Please bill me.

Name__________

Address__________

City_____ State_____ Zip_____

____

(your signature to prevent unauthorized use)

(Orders outside U.S. must include payment in U.S. funds. Add $2.00 per year for postage.)

Advertisement for *Aspen* magazine, from *The New York Times*, October 1967.

14 For more information on *Aspen* (1965 to 1971) see www.ubu.com/aspen/

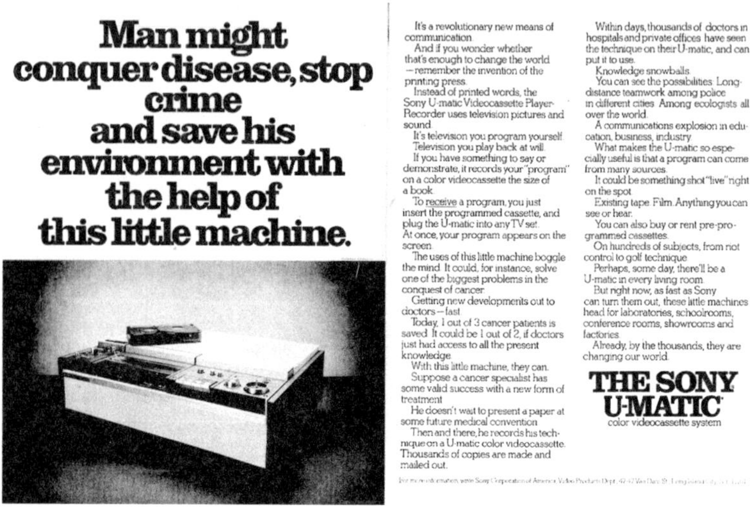

Advertisement for the Sony U-Matic Color Videocassette System, *Time Magazine*, 1973.

interested in: capturing the zeitgeist, profiling certain ideas about production. In a way this was also the goal of *Aspen*, and there are of course many similarities between the two projects: different editors for each issue; the contributions were often either fragments from a larger work or works in progress. And both of them now have something of the time capsule about them. In the case of *Infermental*, because it's U-matic video, the object itself has become effectively useless because the technology is pretty much obsolete — and, unlike *Aspen*, you're unlikely to find back-issues of *Infermental* on eBay, selling for £1,000. But it was never about the object anyway.

George Clark — One of the things that wasn't theorised explicitly was the material condition of *Infermental* — in the way that *Aspen* was really reflective on the material parameters of the magazine or what that could constitute. In the case of *Infermental*, the material of the magazine would change with technology because it was a pile of tapes. But generally the tapes weren't something that the editors had a material relationship to, apart from the fact that each section would last an hour, the duration of one U-matic tape. There was no specificity to the fact that it was a U-matic video tape. There doesn't seem to have been a discussion of the material or technological conditions of the project, in terms of this idea of what a magazine could be.

Will Holder — So the *Infermental* editors hadn't found a means to broadcast or distribute it at the beginning?

George Clark — There wasn't really a way to produce an issue that would be as portable and as distributable as they had hoped it would be …

Dan Kidner — But what they were trying to do was build an alternative network for this work. And in a way they were utilising — while at the same time sitting outside of — a network of institutions. Though they didn't have a critical concept of what it would mean to occupy an existing network, or to build a new one. And for me this is crucial to what makes *Infermental* unique, and potentially instructive when thinking about the current possibility for moving-image production and distribution: this desire to build new image-spaces. There is a sense in which many discussions around moving-image production now are still wedded, or have become reconnected, to film theoretical discourses from the 1970s, but many of these theories don't hold because the spaces where independent film production is seen are not the same. As with all moving images, it is theoretically possible — if you have the DVDs, or digital files — to watch the issues of *Infermental* at home, on the bus, on big screens, on small screens, on computer screens, and so on.

This brings us onto one of the other key issues: the technological conditions of possibility for this

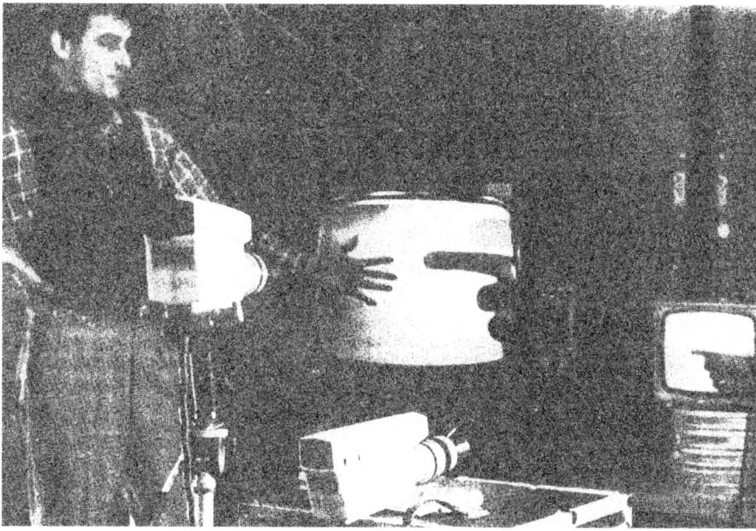

Gabór Bódy shooting *Four Bagatelles* c.1974, from *Bódy Gabór 1946–1985, A Presentation of His Work*, eds. László Beke, Miklós Peternák (1987, Budapest: Mucsarnok).

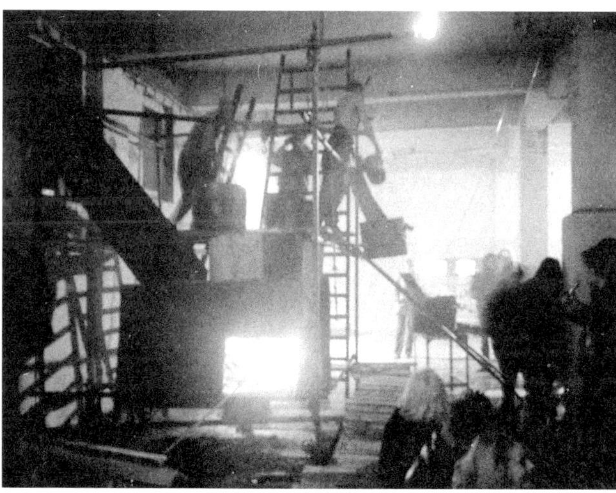

Feu Parfait, multimedia performance, Amsterdam (c. 1985), photo courtesy Gérard Couty.

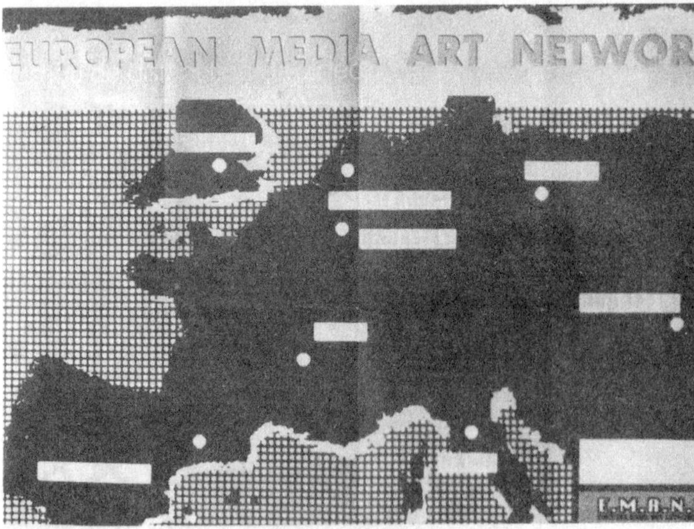

European Media Art Network/EMAN poster, c.1985, from *Bódy Gabór 1946–1985, A Presentation of His Work*, eds. László Beke, Miklós Peternák (1987, Budapest: Mucsarnok), p. 333.

15
The European Media Art Network (E.M.A.N), initiated by Frigo, Lyon, came out from various groups involved in *Infermental* and video art in the early 1980s. On 26/27 September 1985 they organised 'Parallel Screenings', with organisations in eight European cities who simultaneously presented each other's one hour video anthologies. Organisations involved in E.M.A.N. included: *Infermental* in Berlin; London Video Arts in London; Beurschouwburg in Brussels; Videographia in Barcelona; Montevideo in Amsterdam; Video Software in Rome; Frigo in Lyon; Tarsulas Studio in Budapest.

project. One of the interesting things we both found when we started looking at *Infermental* was the rhetoric around the project, which echoes the types of things that were regularly said about the internet in the 1990s. Or at least by artists and cultural producers who saw it as facilitating a new way to distribute their work — in a way liberated from the established institutions.

One of Bódy's big ideas was simultaneous presentation, and he attempted this with another project called European Media Networks in 1985.[15] But, practically, the way that something like this was possible was to have different audiences around the world linked by telephone and people stationed in front of video players pressing play at the same time. So their ideas were always playing catch-up with technology. Technology has now caught up with their ideas, and in many ways eclipsed them. Or rather technology has made their ideas, and wildest dreams, possible.

George Clark There is also a discussion around broadcast at this time and the idea that television was starting to open up to different types of work. There was this real feeling that filmmakers who'd been working solely in the cinema would have another way to generate income for their work, and space to show it.

Will Holder But *Infermental* was never broadcast — it wasn't television …

Dan Kidner No, but a lot of video artists were thinking about the idea of broadcasting as a different way of distributing their work. It is interesting because, for many film collectives and political filmmakers in the 1970s, film was seen as the privileged mode for getting messages across to a broad audience, generate discussion afterwards and subsequently mobilise them. Socially, television was seen to promote passivity and compliance — it still is, of course.

But the way video and media artists began to think about distribution was through the idea of broadcasting. Whether this was television or not, they're still thinking about a more dislocated or dispersed form of distribution and presentation. Of course this also goes back, in some respects, to Gerry Schum's 1969 *Land Art* project, and to Nam June Paik. Not to mention Wolf Vostell's early films, which reworked television programmes ...[16]

Although it was important for political filmmakers in the 1970s to be present at screenings, video artists in the 1980s generally had a different understanding of the potential role of audiences. And broadcasting was sometimes simply seen as a way to get work to a large number of people.

George Clark But there are all of these contradictory positions within that. Some people are interested in TV purely as a means to get their work

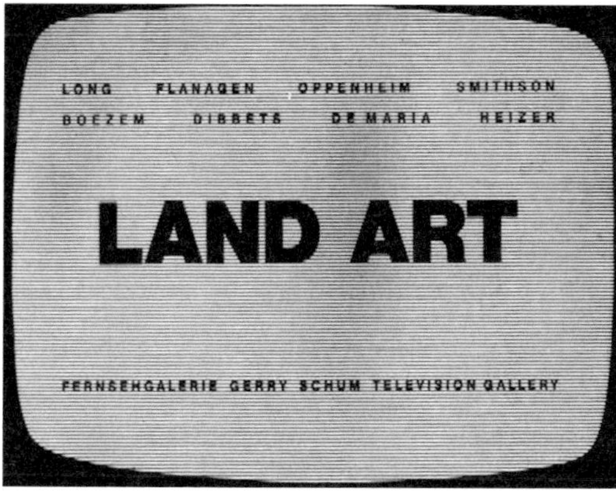

Gerry Schum, 'Television Gallery', 1968 to 1969 Catalogue, 1969, © Gerry Schum.

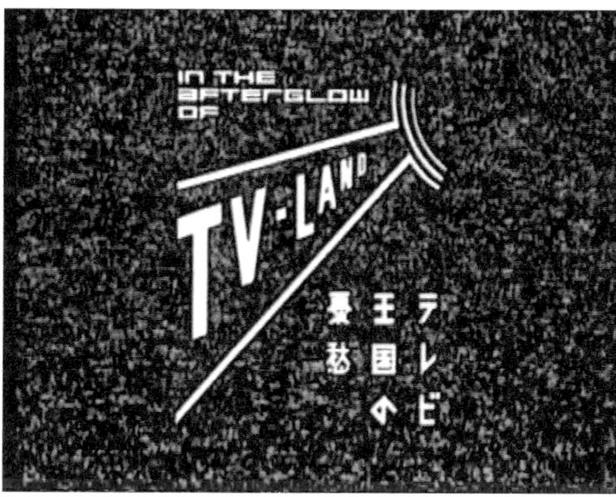

Infermental 8: Toyko, Japan, 1988, edited by Keiko Sei and Alfred Birnbaum and supervised by Mike Hentz and Hank Bull. This edition had the title 'In The Afterglow of TV-Land' and sought to 'focus on television culture via five themes, comic to critical, literal to metaphonic.' [Alfred Birnbaum].

16
In the late 1960s Gerry Schum (1938 to 1973) developed his concept of a 'Television Gallery' as a new means of distribution for contemporary art. He produced two major exhibitions on TV: 'Land Art' (1968 to 1969) for Sender Freies Berlin/ADR and 'Identifications' for SWF Baden-Baden in 1970. He declared at the time that: 'Art should no longer be made for the privacy or exclusiveness of dealers or collectors […] Until now artists have not succeeded in finding a modern system of communication. The only chance I see for the visual arts is the conscious deployment of television.' For more information see www.medienkunstnetz.de/works/land-art/

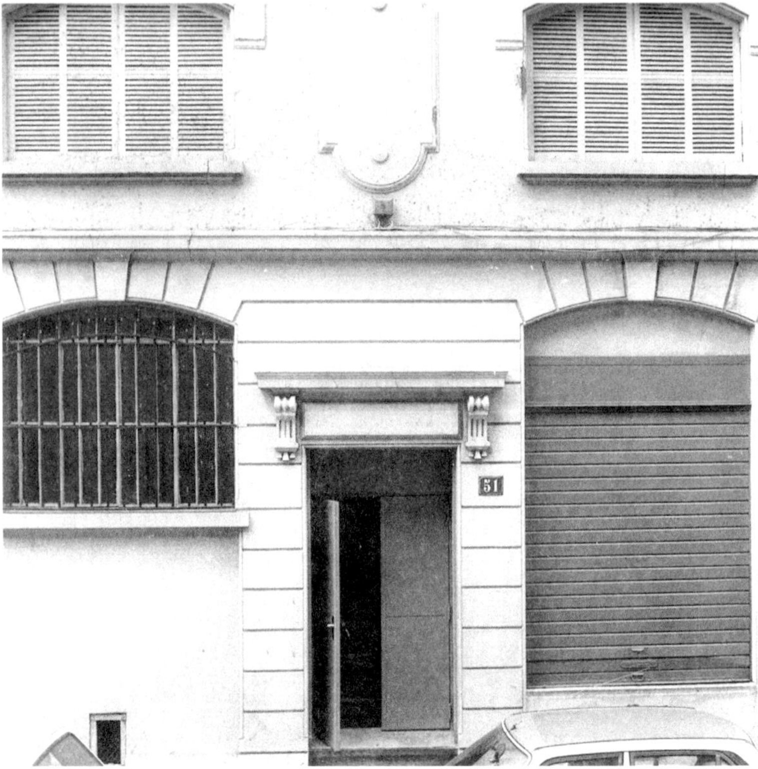

Frigo entrance, Lyon, France, photo courtesy Gérard Couty.

17
Frigo edited *Infermental 4*. The group consisted of Gérard Couty, Mike Hentz, Christian Vanderborght and was founded in 1978 as a new media 'platform' in Lyon, containing a 'cultural lab', a video gallery, exhibition space, an artists in residence programme, and a pirate radio station.

to the largest possible audience, while others had a very different conception of television, seeing it as a way to generate a certain amount of revenue. There were also these new hierarchies being built around who had access to what technology.

You had this split discourse: on one side video was theorised as this democratic medium, but very quickly positions were being taken that excluded a huge amount of people because of access to technology. Already there was a highly developed discourse around a certain type of use of this emerging technology that some people now argue was exclusive, in that it required the support of certain institutions.

Dan Kidner You also had organisations like Frigo,[17] which edited *Infermental 4* in 1985. Frigo was very different to the new media institutions we have now (ZKM in Karlsruhe, FACT in Liverpool, and so on). They came out of a DIY culture with a punk sensibility. Not just in terms of the aesthetic, but also in terms of how to get work made and how to get it out there — how you get an audience for it. Frigo was an artists' group that ran their own art centre in Lyon, where they also had a radio station, a performance space and U-matic editing equipment. So their issue was the first for which the editors had independent access to that technology.

In a way it's hard to talk about comparable projects, because *Infermental* was so unique, but you could think about this DIY culture in terms of video. In the UK, something like Scratch Video springs to mind, which was roughly contemporary with *Infermental*, but which utilised a much more informal way of distributing work on VHS tapes through record shops.[18]

George Clark In some ways with Scratch Video you could argue there was more self-consciousness about the material, because at this time you could already record onto a VHS tape. So artists could sell their tapes in a record store and parallel the emergence of dance music compilations and things like that, but it's a very culturally specific type of project whereas *Infermental*'s ambitions were global.

Dan Kidner And although Bódy called it a 'magazine' it was actually more like an event. In order to watch an issue of *Infermental* in the 1980s you really had to go to an organised screening, and sit for five or six hours.

George Clark The ICA in London did actually have a video library,[19] and so you could consult the videos at your leisure — but you're right, the primary mode of exhibition was the event.

Dan Kidner When we first spoke to Vera Baksa-Soós, Bódy's widow, we were really interested in

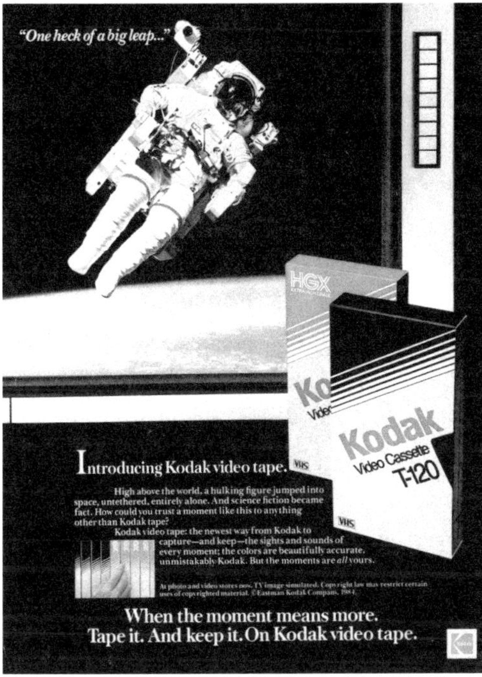

Kodak VHS Video Casette advert from *The Financial Post Magazine*, July 1, 1984.

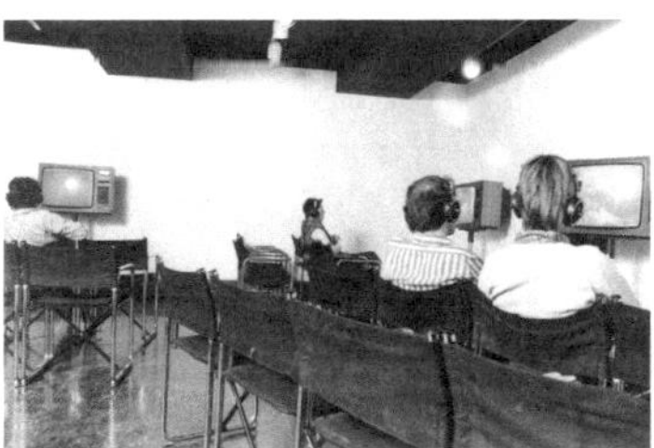

ICA Video Library in use, c.1981.

18
Greatest Hits of Scratch Video Volume 1 was released in 1984 and *Volume 2* in 1985. www.luxonline.org.uk/artists/george_barber/the_greatest_hits_of_scratch_video.html

19
In 1981 the ICA opened the Cinematheque and Video Library. Open to members to watch films and tapes, the Video Library had a growing collection of artist tapes with work by Derek Jarman, Bill Viola, Ian Breakwell, John Jost, Nam June Paik and many others.

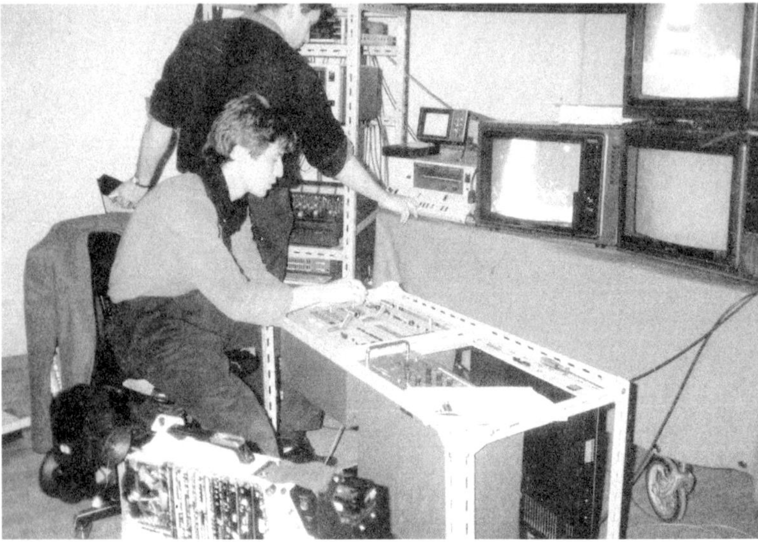

Frigo video studio, Lyon, France, c.1985, photo courtesy Gérard Couty.

the mode of presentation, because we couldn't find any documentation about exactly how the issues were presented. She emphasised that it was incredibly important that they were shown from beginning to end, and this would more often than not be on a monitor, especially in the early years. So you'd have a whole group of people huddled around a TV set for five hours …

George Clark

But it's also important to understand what would constitute a public presentation for this project. Bódy's ambition was for the project to be an encyclopaedia, in that he was gathering reference material: it was this latent sense of the encyclopaedia, the fact that these tapes would then be available for people to refer back to, that meant *Infermental*'s public wasn't necessarily immediate. Yet in some ways this aspect was the most underdeveloped part of the project, largely because of the limits of technology, and also because of the institutions that existed.

Infermental was primarily screened at festivals, where it might be shown on a scheduled day, or shown during the day and people would come in and out. But because of the limits of the technology — for example, someone would have to change the tape on the hour — it couldn't be shown unattended. This is something that we can do now, and did for the Focal Point Gallery exhibition in 2010. But also there was not really the idea at that time that a

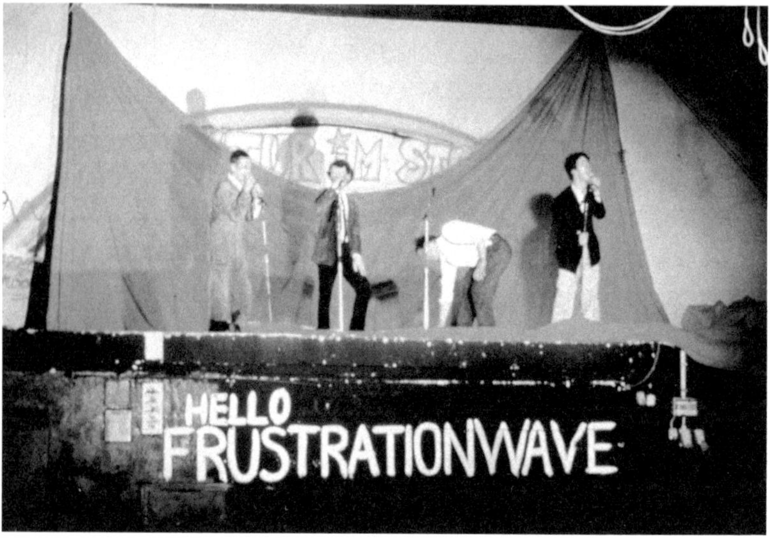

Concert in Beirut by members of Frigo/Minus Delta T, c. 1983, photo Gérard Couty.

20
In various documents and press releases as well as the poster for issues 3 and 4 of *Infermental* Gábor Bódy is credited as 'Initiator'.

continuous looped presentation might actually be a desirable thing.

Infermental was also understood along the lines of the idea of 'new opera' that emerged in the 1980s, whereby opera and new media had this weird relationship, and some thought that opera would be renewed through the use of technology. When Gérard Couty, one of the founders of Frigo, was showing me stills from various projects he was almost embarrassed at how opulent some of the events were.

Dan Kidner — Certainly a lot of the bands in Berlin at that time also had this operatic idea of what pop music could be.

George Clark — There's also this connection to an early theorisation of the music video …

Dan Kidner — That's true.

George Clark — … and the way that the music video then changed the idea of performance style and the importance of the image of a pop band or a group. The constitution of *Infermental* as a collective project is also important: although there was always quite a clear sense that Bódy initiated the project,[20] every issue was edited by multiple people, with one editor from the previous issue acting as a supervisor.

The origins of *Infermental* are slightly uncertain. And because Gábor Bódy died in 1986, there is an absence at the centre of the project; even though it was a collective project, he was seen as the figurehead — the only person who could really say what *Infermental* was.

Dan Kidner

But I think already even before Gábor died, his wife Vera was basically coordinating the whole project — he was already absent in a way …

George Clark

Gábor was involved in the first few issues, primarily in the first issue and the third issue, but by 1983 he was also making the feature *Dog's Night Song*,[21] and was very busy with other things. So even though everyone says he was the main force, he seems to have inspired people and then let them take it on.

Will Holder

It's a collective venture and therefore it's deauthored and anyone can speak of it and it becomes …

George Clark

It was a collective venture but *Infermental* wasn't the solution … It was a way to try and find, even to establish, a different type of network. People were involved because they thought it might be a good thing that other people could see their video, or else they knew someone involved and it sounded like an interesting project to be part of. But it was never really the ideal environment — their contributions would always exist as a reference

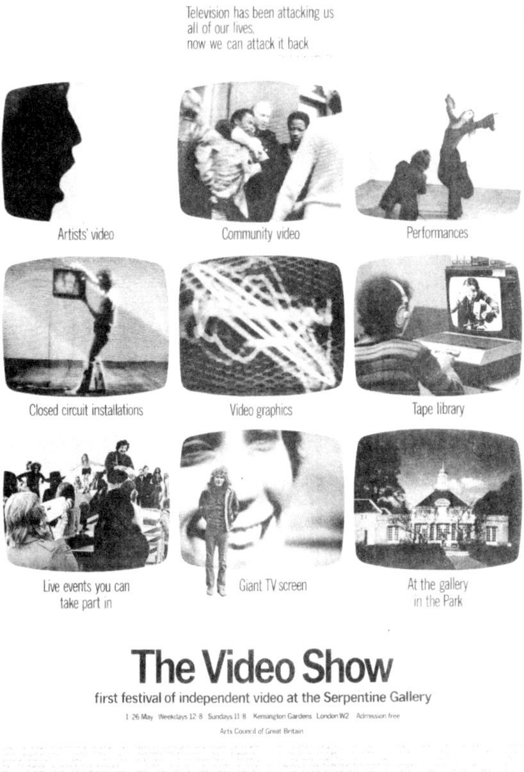

The Video Show, 1975, exhibition catalogue cover, Serpentine Gallery, London.

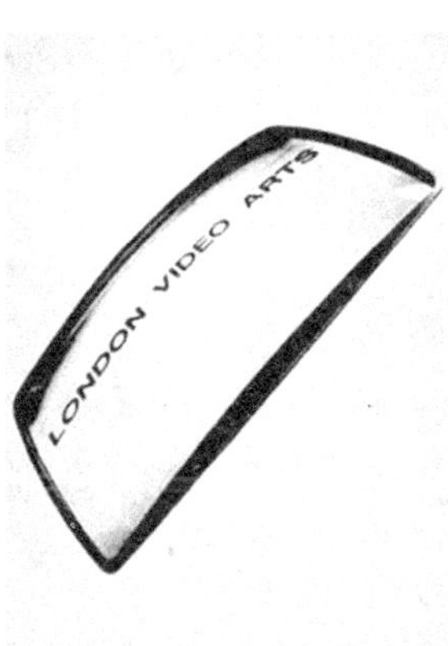

Cover of the first London Video Arts distribution catalogue, 1978, courtesy LUX.

21
Kutya éji dala (Dog's Night Song, 1983).

22
For a short history of London Video Arts (LVA), founded in 1976, see www.luxonline.org.uk/history/1970-1979/lva_founded.html

THE VIDEO SHOW — SERPENTINE GALLERY

LIVE EVENTS

INSTALLATION PROGRAMME

1–9	May	Trevor Pollard	Ghost Piece
1–7	May	David Hall	Progressive Recession
7–10	May	Roger Barnard	Video Corridor
10–11	May	Action Space	Frozen Moment
11–15	May	Brian Hoey	Videvent
13–14	May	Su Braden	3 Views from the Park
16–19	May	Nigel Smith	Thoughts across a Spark Plug
16–18	May	Mike Leggett	Outside the Grounds of Obscenity and Inside the Grounds of Hyde Park
20–21	May	SURPRISE EVENT	
21–26	May	David Hall/Tony Sinden	101 TV Sets
22–24	May	Su Braden	3 Views from the Park

PERFORMANCES

1 May	6.30–7.30	Dirk Larsen	The Nesral Krid Echt
	6.00–8.00	Videoart Group	Videodance Perspectives
2 May	5.30–7.30	Bill Lundberg	The First Conversation
3 May	4.30–7.30	Cliff Evans	Electric Newspaper
	3.00–5.00	Mike Dunford	Blind Circuit
	All day	Phantom Captain	in garden
4 May	7.00–7.30	Tamara Krikorian	Breeze
	5.30–7.30	Stuart Marshall	Analysis of a Suicide
	All day	Inter-Action	Community Media Van
5 May	7.00–7.30	Rolande Thomas & others	Set Piece for One Performance
	5.30–7.30	North East London Polytechnic	Encounter with Video
6 May	5.30–7.30	SURPRISE EVENT	
7 May	6.30–7.30	Tony Sinden	Video Vacuum
8 May	5.30–7.30	North East London Polytechnic	Encounter with Video
9 May	7.00–7.30	David Critchley	Another Triangle
10 May	All day	Inter-Action	Community Media Van
	7.00–7.30	Rolande Thomas & others	Set Piece for One Performance
11 May	5.30–7.30	Bill Lundberg	The First Conversation
12 May	5.30–7.30	North East London Polytechnic	Encounter with Video
13 May	5.00–7.00	Mike Dunford	Blind Circuit
	6.30–7.30	Tony Sinden	Video Vacuum
14 May	7.00–7.30	Tamara Krikorian	Breeze
	4.30–7.30	Cliff Evans	Electric Newspaper
15 May	5.30–7.30	North East London Polytechnic	Encounter with Video
16 May	5.30–7.30	Stuart Marshall	Analysis of a Suicide
	7.00–7.30	David Critchley	Another Triangle
17 May	All day	Phantom Captain	Hand-held Follies of 1975
	4.30–7.30	John Hopkins	You Can Make it if you Try
	6.00–7.00	Dirk Larsen	The Nesral Krid Echt
18 May	All day	Phantom Captain	Hand-held Follies of 1975
	6.00–7.00	Rolande Thomas & others	Set Piece for One Performance
19 May	5.30–7.30	North East London Polytechnic	Encounter with Video
20 May	5.30–7.30	Videoart Group	Videodance Perspective
21 May	7.00–7.30	Tamara Krikorian	Breeze
22 May	7.00–7.30	Rolande Thomas & others	Set Piece for One Performance
	6.30–7.30	Dirk Larsen	The Nesral Krid Echt
23 May	5.30–7.30	Bill Lundberg	The First Conversation
24 May	All day	Inter-Action	Community Media Van
	6.00–7.00	Tony Sinden	Video Vacuum
25 May	All day	Inter-Action	Community Media Van
		Dogg's Troupe	TV Whee
	All day	Phantom Captain	Hand-held Follies of 1975
	5.30–7.30	Videoart Group	Videodance Perspectives
26 May	All day	Phantom Captain	Hand-held Follies of 1975
	3.00–5.00	Mike Dunford	Blind Circuit
	4.30–7.30	Cliff Evans	Electric Newspaper

SPECIAL INTEREST SCREENINGS

9 May	3.00–8.00	Artists' tapes
13 May	3.00–8.00	Women's tapes
19 May	3.00–8.00	Open Screening
22 May	3.00–8.00	Community Television: introduced by George Stoney

The Video Show 1–26 May 1975 open daily 12–8 Sundays 11–8 admission free Serpentine Gallery Kensington Gardens W2

'The Video Show', 1975, live events programme, Serpentine Gallery, London.

23 For more information on 'The Video Show', Serpentine Gallery, 1975, see www.luxonline.org.uk/history/1970-1979/the_video_show.html

to the work, yet the real version would exist somewhere else.

There is something interesting about the relationship to the UK and to British discourses. There was a lot of dialogue with London Video Arts,[22] and there was some discussion about doing a British issue. But it was one of the few active places where it didn't happen, despite there being quite a lot of British video artists — such as George Barber, Judith Goddard, Richard Grayson, Tony Morgan and John Scarlett-Davis — included in the early issues of *Infermental*. But the UK was not really part of this German discourse around new media, or part of this relationship between Hungary and Germany.

Dan Kidner Well it's almost more related to a mid-1970s discourse around video, which is just getting going at the time of 'The Video Show' at the Serpentine Gallery in 1975.[23] There were similar utopian ideas about video and how this new technology might enable artists to network themselves and their work in a different way. But I think that, by the early 1980s, moving-image production in the UK is very different.

Will Holder Dan, maybe this is a good point to talk about your own personal research interests, and those of James Richards in relation to this. What kind of interest can be generated in the UK for an exhibition about a project like *Infermental*, and why now?

Dan Kidner

Well, George and I were working on similar things but from different perspectives. Initially we talked about doing a project about video art together. George was already looking into the history of *Infermental*, which at that point was not a project I knew anything about.

George Clark

In some ways *Infermental* is not very well documented or often referenced within English-language video art discourses, even though the tapes were at the ICA. They were later donated to the British Artists Film and Video Study Collection at Central Saint Martins in London,[24] which is where I first watched them.

If you talk to German curators, there is an awareness of the particular generation that was involved in *Infermental*. It still has a certain presence there — especially on the festival circuit. And at new media festivals like Transmediale in Berlin and Ars Electronica in Linz.[25]

Dan Kidner

At the point when we decided to do something around *Infermental*, I had been looking at political film in the 1970s and 1980s for a while, and specifically at the development of the form of the essay film. I was also looking at the history of British film collectives.

24
For more information on the British Artists' Film and Video Study Collection see www.studycollection.co.uk/

25
Various issues of *Infermental* were presented at both festivals during the 1980s. *Infermental* 7 was produced in Buffalo, USA, and supported in part by the Ars Electronica Festival, Linz, Austria 1987. This issue was edited by the Austrian artist and curator Peter Weibel who was the artistic advisor to Ars Electronica during this time. In 2007 Transmediale presented a retrospective of *Infermental* with excerpts from all the issues and presentations and discussions with the original editors. This was organised by The Concrete Narrative Society e.V. — Katja Pratschke and Gusztáv Hámos.

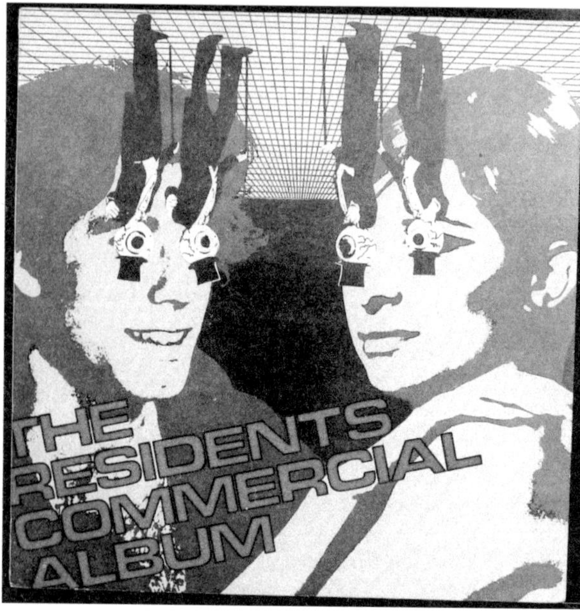

The Residents *Commercial Album*, released by Ralph Records, USA, 1980.

George Clark

I'd been involved in organising a retrospective of the feature film director Miklós Jancsó at the Riverside Studios, London, in 2003, and through my research for that I came across the Béla Belázs Studio, and got really interested in the history of experimental film in Hungary, and Gábor Bódy's work in particular. The breadth of his work is not really known or understood: he is often cited, yet only as an eccentric but influential filmmaker, whose work was still speculative because his career ended quite abruptly.

Dan Kidner

I was interested in a set of questions around the efficacy of certain tropes and strategies used by political filmmakers in the mid- to late-1970s, as well as their aesthetic appropriation by contemporary filmmakers. Hanging over all this was a question about how different notions of collectivity were embodied in the films themselves, but also the modes of distribution and presentation. So in our early conversations about *Infermental* I wanted to think about this idea of what it meant to build a community around the moving image and what kinds of collective production were involved. These were my inroads into the project.

In terms of how James became involved, I guess after a few months of George and I talking about the potential for a project about *Infermental* we began to think about how we might present it in a gallery. There were a lot of presentational issues involved and we decided that it would be interesting to work with an artist on developing some kind of architectural structure within which we could re-present all of the editions, or a number of them. We knew James' work and were interested in a piece he had made called *Active Negative Programme* (2008), which took the form of a film programme presented on a monitor. The monitor and several rows of chairs were placed on a platform. This mode of presentation really interested us, because it at once created this distance from the gallery and made you aware of your place within it.

Also, aesthetically, James seemed to be recasting the idea of the compilation film, which as a method was quite prevalent in the early editions of *Infermental*. Gusztáv Hámos and Christoph Dreher's work in particular, whose video from *Infermental 1*, *Commercials* (1981), consists of a compilation of clips taken from the television and set to the music of The Residents.[26]

Our very first idea, before James was involved, was to actually make a contemporary version of *Infermental*. But I think that was jettisoned almost as soon as we started to think about the problems of working with an existing archive.

George Clark Our original sense of the project was that it was an archive. The use of, and interest in archives within film and visual art practice and discourse really came later. We felt that James' mode

26
A ten-minute extract of *Commercials — 40 One-Minute Adventures in the World of TV* (43min, video, 1981) by Gusztáv Hámos and Christoph Dreher is included in *Infermental 1* (1982). The video was made from more than thirty hours of television from both the West German (FRG) and East German (DDR) stations available in Berlin.

of working was very much related to this tendency, but in a way that was quite distinct from how filmmakers had been using found material in the 1980s.

One way we felt we could approach the project, was by treating *Infermental* as a proposal or template that we could simply continue. We did start to discuss which artists we would include in a contemporary edition.

Dan Kidner But immediately we knew that it would be very difficult because of how things had shifted. It would have been on such a different scale and so much more complicated in terms of contemporary artists' relationships with their commercial galleries and distributors.

George Clark It was an important part of the original concept of *Infermental* that it would include a range of work — from performance to video pieces — made using a variety of formats: everything from 35mm and 8mm to video, in that *Infermental* was a meeting place for different practices that usually wouldn't share the same space.

Dan Kidner In terms of the technology it would be easy to do it now — everything would fit onto one, or a number of DVDs, and it would be cheap and easy to distribute. Or everything could be uploaded to the internet and streamed or made available for download. But there are many artists working now

D E C L A R A T I O N

1. I declair that I keep all rights, incl. musicrights, of my contribution for the second INFERMENTAL edition.

2. I agree that I get my righteous part of 50% of the income - divided in same parts among all participants.

3. For special causes, festivals, didactic institutions, I agree that INFERMENTAL will be presented for free -

4. I take cognizance of the fact that I will be informed about all presentations of IF 2/82 (place/institution/ income/sucsess) within the first of Juli 1983.

5. I have to get back my original-material within the first of december 1982.

date...................... signature...........................

Name/adress/bankaccount :

Please inform us about renewal suggestions, possibilities of distribution, good ideas, good people.

Original artists declaration form for inclusion in *Infermental*, document from ZKM archive, c. 1981/1982.

with the moving image who are very specific about modes of presentation and formats. For example, there are artists working within the gallery who shoot on 16mm, and will only show their work projected. For those artists it is crucial that their work is seen in that way, and there is no sense in which they'd be happy for the work to be compressed into a digital file, and compiled on a disc with a bunch of films by other artists.

George Clark — Prior to *Infermental*, in discussions around structural/materialist film, these positions were largely defined in relation to cinema. This materialist critique of the cinematic apparatus is hard to sustain now that there are so many different modes of presentation, not just one.

Dan Kidner — This is an important point. But this materialist position does persist in some practices, however hollow it may seem. The question is, what would be the benefit of squeezing all of these different practices into one format, with little or no possibility for determining how the material is watched?

Will Holder — Exactly. But at the same time, in order to unpick the complicated nature of this from every single perspective, it almost does help to say that at one point we considered this list of artists, but why doesn't that work, or why is that so much more complicated now?

Dan Kidner I don't know if it would definitely not work … The thing was, at a certain point, we decided that an anthology or a contemporary version of the 'video magazine' wasn't the most interesting way to interrogate the project.

Now the question is: in what way did *Infermental* successfully represent a cross-section of production, and what did it mean to represent rather than present artwork? As George suggested, the project was arguably only possible if the contributor submitted to their work being 'represented' on the tapes — contemporary moving-image practitioners, generally, wouldn't be as comfortable having their work used in this way.

George Clark *Infermental* especially intrigued us also because it engaged with all sorts of production, from performance videos through to video diaries, ethnographic documentary material, music videos …

Dan Kidner But because our project tried to provide these layered, multiple perspectives, on the uses of the moving image within contemporary art institutions, it is important in this respect to take into account what happened after the 1980s. This is when you see the rise of film installation, and what more recently has been given the generic term, 'artists' film and video', which was predominantly a very formal

What is INFERMENTAL (IF)

IF is an international Periodicum on Videotapes with innovating aspects for art and communication.

IF publishes works within a range of 10 minutes:

1.) Original works produced on video specially for IF
2.) Documentaries about innovating visual events
3.) Films which don't lose their character when copied on video in order to give information about their existence
4.) Parts of a film (trailer) for publicity of the filmmakers

Planning for distribution:

1) Hire
2) Selling the copies
3) lending to cultural institutions who have not got much money on a non-profit base

We are thinking of meetings of the filmmakers involved f.ex. after a presentation on a filmfestival having exchanges about organisation and development of IF

contact: Gábor Bódy
Uhlandstr. 184
1 Berlin 12
030/ 883 8664

'What is *Infermental*?' document from ZKM archive, c. 1981/1982.

way of understanding the moving image. A lot of this work responded primarily to the cinematic image, and brought cinematic images into the gallery to examine them — sometimes critically, often not. And the possibility of doing that is predicated on having available different technologies of projection. I think it's wrong sometimes to think of that kind of work as actually existing in the same continuum as video art — in a way you could argue that it is a completely different art form.

George Clark You could also argue that many practices are excluded from the gallery due to what you could call ahistorical discussions of artists using film and video. I mean that there is an ongoing reappraisal of certain experimental filmmakers and video artists who have been written into a canon and whose work is understood through the prism of 'artists' film and video' as it has been understood in the field of contemporary art since the 1990s. So people as diverse as Tony Conrad, Morgan Fisher and Chantal Akerman have had their work rehabilitated in a way to fit into the contemporary art market.

But at the same time I believe there is a shift now to a broader understanding of film and video practice, as seen in artists' engagement with event-based presentation rather than just installations and in the production of long-form work that is maybe more socially sited or reflective.

Dan Kidner

Absolutely, and that work is, in a way, more connected to the video art of the 1980s and the political, long-form essay or montage film of the 1970s and early 1980s, than it is to the work of the 1990s. From Emily Wardill to Anja Kirschner and David Panos through to artists such as Hito Steyerl, these practices are also engaged with more mainstream or other types of image production. The crucial difference between these and earlier practices is that neither the images themselves nor the cinematic apparatus are now seen as necessarily ideological.

George Clark

I think our presentation of *Infermental* was a way to reflect on this contemporary re-engagement with a broader understanding of the sites and histories of film and video inside and outside of the gallery. But then in some ways the contemporary gallery has become the institution that *Infermental* proposed.

Dan Kidner

This is an important point. Firstly *Infermental* was propositional — the technology was always lagging behind the ideas — and the real conditions of possibility for the project are only now with us. But the contemporary art gallery now is also the site for experimental — or what you might call 'advanced' — moving-image practices; the way that galleries are networked and technologically equipped for these practices could be seen as the triumph of the moving image over other forms of contemporary art.

This was something about our exhibition at Focal Point Gallery that I think many people didn't pick up on — there was this strong sense of melancholy that ran through it. There is a sense in which Gábor Bódy's dream was realised: it was realised by the internet, but also by the gallery in the way that it can now present all media within its walls. But I really don't think this is exactly what he wanted — this isn't what he dreamt of.

Will Holder Films and DVDs on loop, walk in and out as you please …

Dan Kidner In some sense, the future that *Infermental* anticipated did come about, but it's wrong somehow. I think in some way we built these structures on platforms to obstruct immersion in this material as much as to facilitate it. Visitors to the gallery were able to approach the presentation in two ways: you could sit down and watch an awful lot of material and really get a sense of the project, or you could step off the platform and have a look at these structures and think about the history — or histories — of moving images migrating to the gallery space.

So at the most pessimistic level you can think through ideas about how the gallery is in some way a mausoleum for the moving image — it's where moving images are put to rest.

George Clark — We wanted to present *Infermental* in a way that was very different to how ZKM had archived it and exhibited it in 2006.[27] We deliberately didn't annotate the material.

Will Holder — You consciously chose to present it without the context — that's the result of the presentation in that sense. People can't consume without the context, or without contextualisation.

George Clark — We weren't aware of withholding context as such. The context is not really accessible — there isn't really a context anymore. *Infermental* is cut loose from those things. It's an archive that hasn't been archived, and that's part of the attraction: because it's a relatively undocumented project, that distance is exciting because it still feels very open.

It feels like there is a desire to understand and to contain *Infermental* at the moment — particularly in Germany. But to do that is maybe to misunderstand it because, in a way, it is still active. Maybe *Infermental* has a polemical element that has intensified with time. For all its editorial structures and frameworks, it's still really ungraspable.

27
Between 7 September and 9 October 2006 ZKM presented the exhibition 'Infermental: Video Vocabulary of the 1980s' in the ZKM Media Lounge. This archival exhibition, curated by Hartmut Jörg, presented all editions of *Infermental* 'now interactively available on a newly created playing station' along with selected original documents from the paper collection donated by Vera Baksa-Soós related to the history of *Infermental*. For more information see http://on1.zkm.de/zkm/stories/storyReader$5260

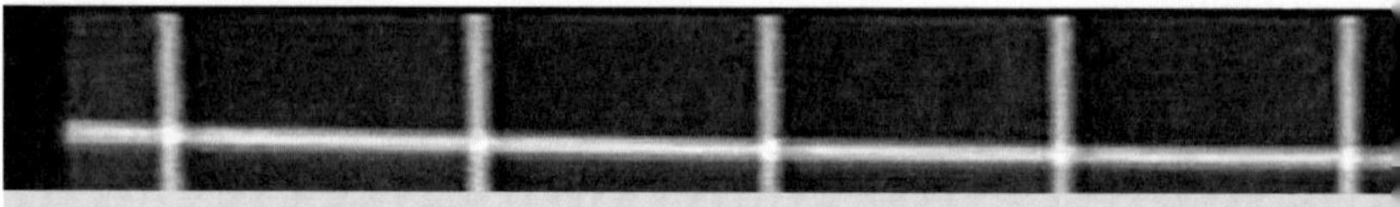

A Detour Around Infermental

Part II
5 April 2011

Dan Kidner
George Clark
James Richards

James Richards: Over the course of working on the 'Infermental' exhibition at Focal Point Gallery, we went from talking about producing timelines and displaying vitrines of ephemera to this really stripped-back show. Things were presented in such a way that they were left as primary material, filtered through a contemporary lens. The three issues of *Infermental* — numbers one, four and eight[1] — as well as the posters, were presented, in a way, like artworks. Or they almost became artworks. I think the way the show evolved like that was interesting — I was really happy with it.

George Clark: I think that process is going to frame this conversation. I guess the thing that I'd be interested in talking about now is how this came about. Maybe you can start by talking about your own interests and work with film and video collections?

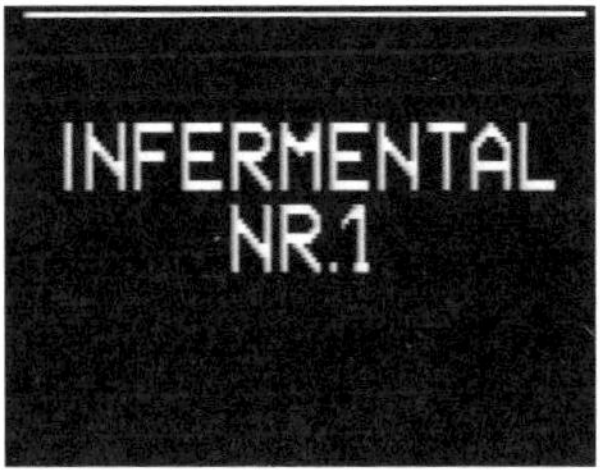

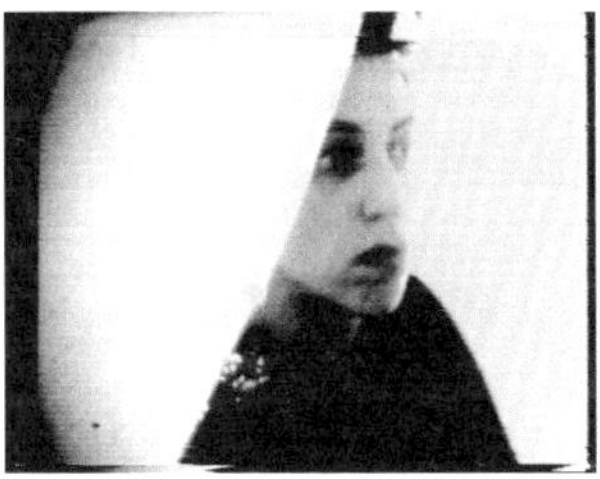

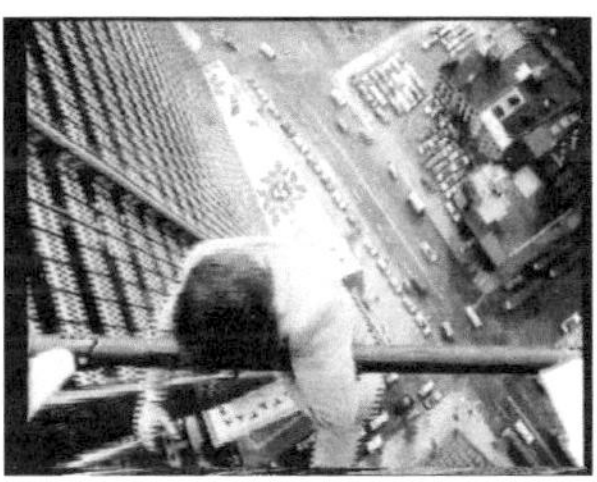

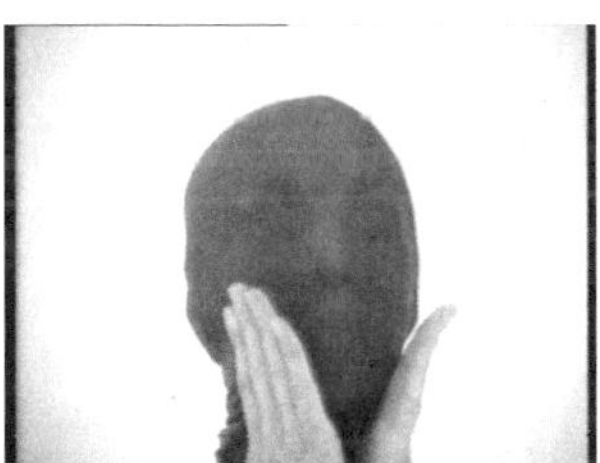

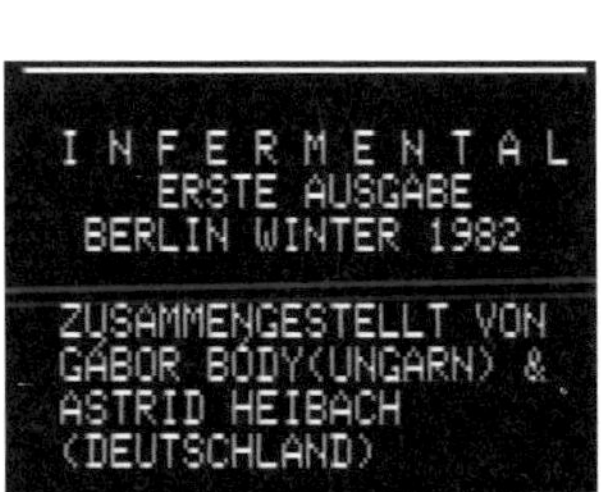

Video stills from *Infermental 1*, Berlin, 1981/1982.

1
Infermental 1, Berlin, 1981/82 (thirty-eight contributions, eight countries, four hours), edited by Gábor Bódy and Astrid Heibach, supervised by Gusztáv Hámos; *Infermental 4*, Lyon, 1985 (one hundred and two contributions, fourteen countries, seven hours), edited by Frigo (Gérard Couty, Mike Hentz, Christian Vanderborght), supervised by Astrid Heibach; *Infermental 8*, Tokyo, 1988 (seventy-three contributions, fifteen countries, five hours), edited by Keiko Sei and Alfred Birnbaum, supervised by Mike Hentz and Hank Bull.

James Richards, installation view, 'Nought To Sixty', ICA, London, 4 to 11 August 2008.

Foreground: *Active Negative Programme*, 2008. Video loop, aluminium platform, chairs and flatscreen.

Background: *Untitled Merchandise (Lovers & Dealers)*, 2007. Six machine knitted nylon blankets, 152 × 228cm.

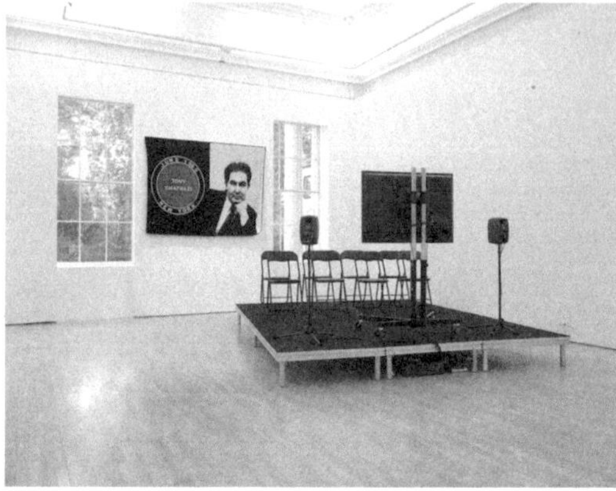

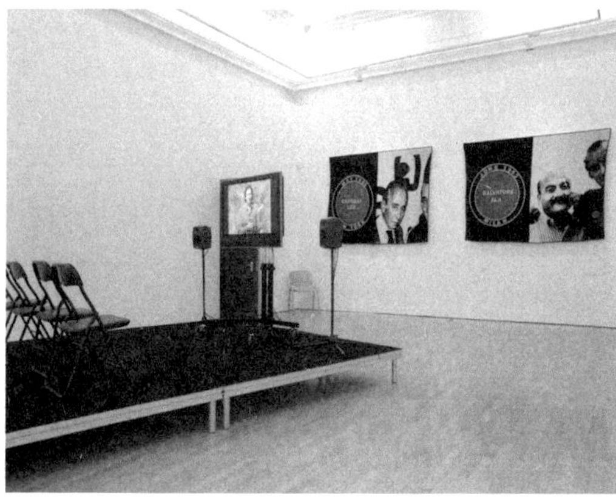

2
LUX is an international arts agency for the support and promotion of artists' moving image practice and the ideas that surround it. Founded in 2002, it is the only organisation of its kind in the UK, represents the country's only significant collection of artists' film and video and is the largest distributor of such work in Europe, representing 4,500 works by approximately 1,500 artists from 1920s to the present day. For more information see www.lux.org.uk

3
James Richards, *Devotion* (2007), 50 min, compiled with material from the LUX archive and the artist's own found footage. First screened at the LUX in June 2007.

4
James Richards, *Active Negative Programme* (2008), 20-minute video programme and installation.

James Richards

I spent a lot of time at LUX watching work, in an unmediated way.[2] You are alone in the screening room, rather than in a gallery where the work has been framed by an artist or a curator. For me, coming from a background making work with found material, I started thinking about how I could creatively play with the screening conditions of works. One of the first projects I did after college was called *Devotion* (2007), which was a curated screening with videos by George Kuchar, Steve Reinke and Anne McGuire, as well as some of my own sequences and some material from friends' camcorders.[3] I mixed it at LUX over an afternoon onto DigiBeta. The programme operated between something curated and something I had made.

I made a piece the following year called *Active-Negative Programme* that continued to experiment with ways of collating material from different sources.[4] There were pieces by Paul Bush and Chris Saunders, but there was also material from the internet as well as fragments of videos and films. The whole thing was made to be shown on a screen, positioned on a platform, with a very particular arrangement of chairs in the space. It became more like a sculpture of a screening, or a sculptural presentation of a screening set-up.

George Clark

The screening room furniture and equipment were appropriated in the same way you might use a fragment of a video in a work …

James Richards

Yes, or at least they were foregrounded or made more theatrical. People had to step up and sit on it. It was first shown upstairs at the ICA in London as part of 'Nought to Sixty' in 2008, in a large room but with quite a small platform, so only eight people could watch at a time. Rather than being in a darkened space they were in the centre of a lit room, watching. So, in a way, everyone involved was very aware of their participation. Another piece that relates to the 'Infermental' project is one I made with Steve Reinke.[5] In 2009 we were asked by Light Industry[6] to curate a programme for their cinema project at X-Initiative's 'No Soul For Sale' event in New York. Steve and I decided that, since we were working and living in separate places, and we had different networks, it'd be interesting to make something together from what we had on our computers. We began by sending material to one another. I sent things that I'd never finished, fragments of existing work and bits of found footage, and he did the same. Then we edited and reworked the material, passing it back and forth. Again, the result sat somewhere between a compilation, or programme, and a work.

George Clark

When we started looking at *Infermental* what sort of parallels did you see with your own practice and projects you'd been involved in?

5
Steve Reinke is a Canadian artist and writer, best known for his works on video. For more information see www.myrectumisnotagrave.com/ and www.blog.musicisplaying.com/

6
Light Industry, founded in 2008, is an independent screening space in Brooklyn, New York, run by Thomas Beard and Ed Halter.

Video stills from *Infermental 4*, Lyon, 1985.

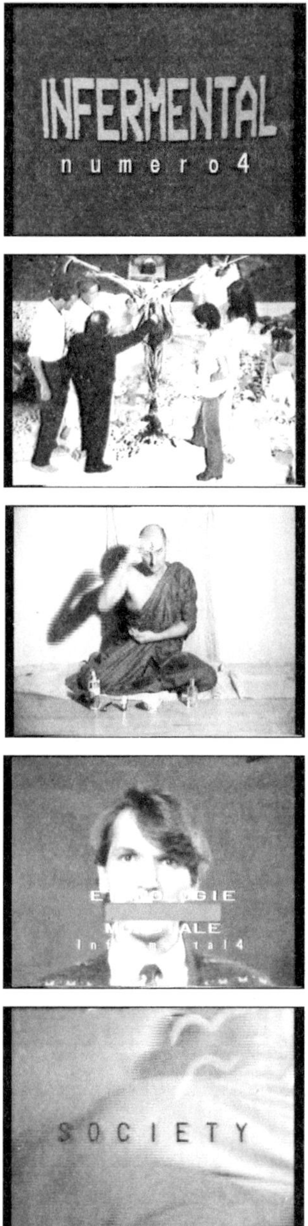

James Richards

The techniques of sampling and compiling used in *Infermental* are familiar to me. I also use these techniques, but we are now at a very different point in terms of the scale and speed of the dispersal of moving images.

Infermental was of course operating at a time when there was a thriving underground film culture. Now culture is more diffuse and, more generally, there is a massive amount of different types of images in circulation from which to sample. But, for example, the free movement between different forms in the Frigo edition in 1985, the way different types of material overlapped — experimental films, documentary, music videos — does relate to the way I compose film programmes.

Dan Kidner

The similarities between James and his generation and this earlier generation of media artists are really interesting. I think James is right when he points to the key difference being the sheer quantity of material available for sampling now. What do we do with this digital detritus? How do we process it and how are the processed images dispersed? The other thing that we flagged up in the earlier conversation was the institutional change: with few exceptions, today's practitioners are hardwired into a quite different system of relations — primarily a system of social relations. James, and others, may sample from this great repository of digital material,

but the question is, into what space are the remixed images inserted?

When we visited ZKM in Karlsruhe early in 2010, and we finally got to watch the editions from beginning to end, the Frigo edition really stood out because of the way it seemed to resonate with the concerns of many artists currently working with film and video.

James Richards Also it was the first edition we watched that we felt was something of its own. We had all watched a lot of programmes of video from the 1970s and 1980s, and the earlier editions seemed quite conventional, as much as there were interesting pieces perhaps or ones that stood out. It felt familiar as a structure. But then with the Frigo edition we saw the editors experimenting with ways of mixing the material and thereby making it quite different from a regular screening of works at a festival, museum or cinema.

George Clark Watching that edition was the tipping point in our understanding of *Infermental*: from previously thinking about it as a screening programme or like Scratch Video, that edition made us realise that the project was totally different. Up to that point a large part of our research had been about trying to get to grips with what *Infermental* was, but putting on an exhibition about the project required a break from that history. We needed to think about how a contemporary presentation could be informed by or relate to these complex histories, and also how to be outside of that and reflect on it critically. How does one accommodate and represent historical research without simply displaying historical documents? That was the big question for me.

Dan Kidner There were issues over what to include and what to leave out. And there were questions about what it would mean to try and 'reactivate' *Infermental*. It is possible to think critically about the then and now if you begin to interrogate the standard modes of presentation of film and video, and of archives, in the gallery space. In the context of an enlarged and more dispersed field of moving-image production the options for its presentation seem disproportionately limited. I'm aware that there is a thriving and growing network of new media practitioners working outside of the art world's very tight network of social relations but, as you say, our aim was in part to see how the discourses of contemporary art filtered these histories of media art, new media art, video art, experimental film, artists' film and video etc …

James Richards And after we spent time at ZKM watching the editions and looking through the printed contracts, posters and documentation of events, we realised that we just wanted to show *Infermental*, and not this other material.

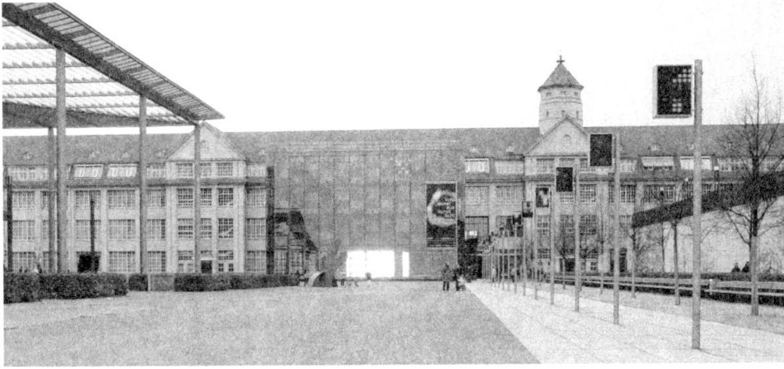

ZKM | Zentrum für Kunst und Medientechnologie/
Center for Art and Media, Karlsruhe, Germany.

Original poster from *Infermental 8*: Toyko, 1988, courtesy ZKM | Center for Art and Media Karlsruhe.

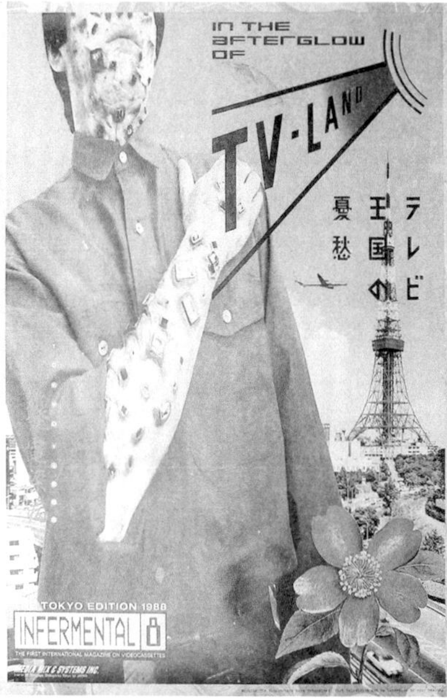

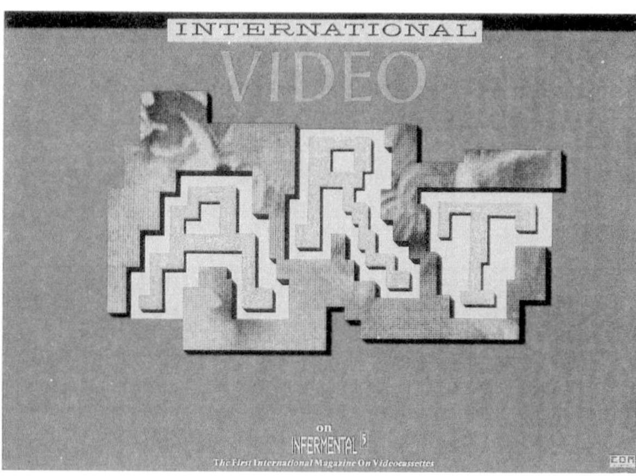

Original poster from *Infermental 5*: Rotterdam, 1986, courtesy ZKM | Center for Art and Media Karlsruhe.

Dan Kidner — But I do think it was much more than simply deciding not to include elements of the archive. It was more about presenting the project with almost no interpretive material, unlike a museum presentation of an archive. Dealing with it as if it wasn't an archive straight away creates a kind of critical distance. This is why we asked you to work on the project, because you were already working with these kinds of distances; compiling existing moving images and filtering them through different systems of presentation.

George Clark — It also throws up this big question about what really constitutes an archive for the moving image. And especially when you're talking about video or new media production, there's a lot of material that went into the *Infermental* tapes, but it can't really be displayed in a simple way. Documents are not necessarily the real archive of *Infermental* – they are only an archive of its administration.

James Richards — Well I suppose *Infermental* was aiming to be its own archive. In itself each edition represents an archive of the different artistic concerns and interests at a given time and even though in each edition there are curated subsections, you still get the sense that the project is more about distributing and documenting, or mapping the range of practices, than making an argument.

Dan Kidner

I wonder if this is true though, about *Infermental* seeking to archive itself: did they have an eye on history in this way? For sure, the stated (and repeated) aim was to chronicle, but in the way a magazine does. I guess there is a tension between the desire to archive and preserve, and the desire to present the here and now.

Other gallery presentations of *Infermental*, most notably the exhibition at ZKM in 2006, paid more attention to ephemera. We very consciously set up this distance between the real material, which would normally be seen to constitute an archive, and the presentational aspects of the project. For example, we reprinted the posters, which in a way constituted a distinct work, on gloss photo paper, rather than showing the originals in frames or making faithful facsimiles. We made high-res scans from the originals, kept their original size, but positioned each one in the centre of identically sized sheets. They were then hung chronologically in a grid. This turned the collection into a wall piece, somehow oscillating between a presentation of artefacts and the creation of a work of art.

James Richards

And, as digital scans, they existed somewhere between a reproduction and a photograph of a poster. They aren't fetishised so heavily in that way, but neither were they shown in a completely transparent way. I suppose, like the tapes themselves,

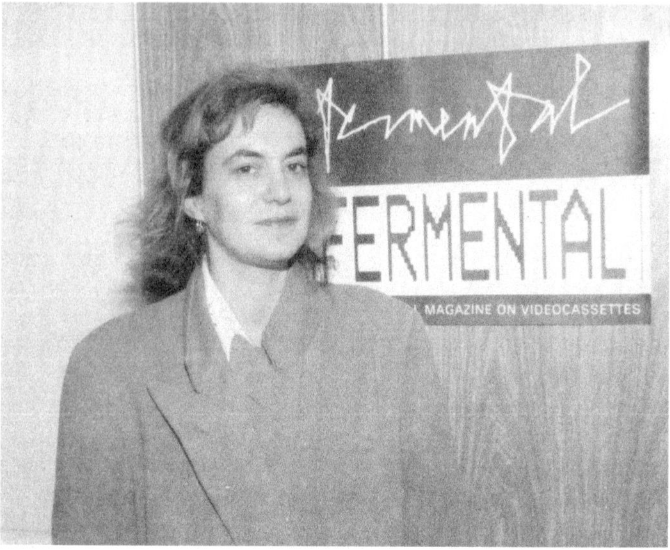

Vera Baksa-Soós with *Infermental* poster at the Berlinale 1987, photo courtesy Vera Baksa-Soós.

Founding document for '*Infermental* — an international recorded imagery project' signed by Hungarian and Polish filmmakers in 1981, document from ZKM archive.

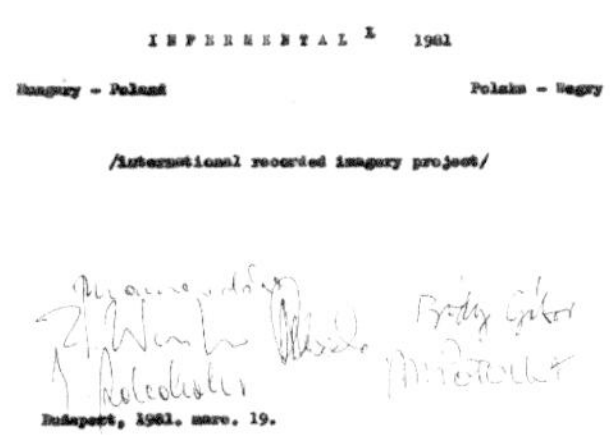

I N F E R M E N T A L 1 1981

Hungary - Poland Polska - Węgry

/International recorded imagery project/

Budapest, 1981. marc. 19.

the posters were made to be public. We were showing things that were intended to be shown rather than showing signed contracts and photographs. It was very much about how the project presented itself and we re-presented and re-staged that. But then it wasn't nostalgic either: the posters were shiny and new — there was something clinical about it.

George Clark

I remember ZKM exhibited a guestbook with signatures from the original *Infermental* screenings. The signed documents from the archive are seen to be the most important. One is this manifesto that was a proposition for *Infermental* that was prepared in Poland in Autumn 1980. It was signed by various attendees. The other is this guestbook. They don't directly relate to *Infermental* unless you understand the project as a proposal.

It's interesting that these documents, in some respects, have more status as objects than the original tapes. During the research period, that was the one thing that we never saw, but is arguably the most important material — these U-matic tapes.

I always imagined that the tapes themselves would be interesting as objects, that they'd have a label or something like that.

James Richards

With a cover, and a graphic, or logo.

Video stills from
Infermental 8, Toyko, 1988.

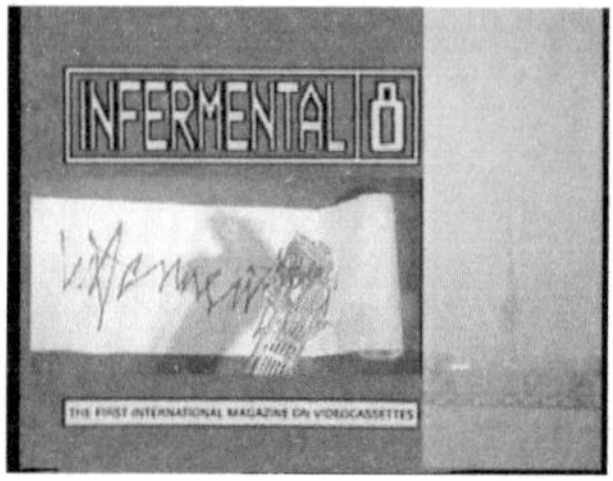

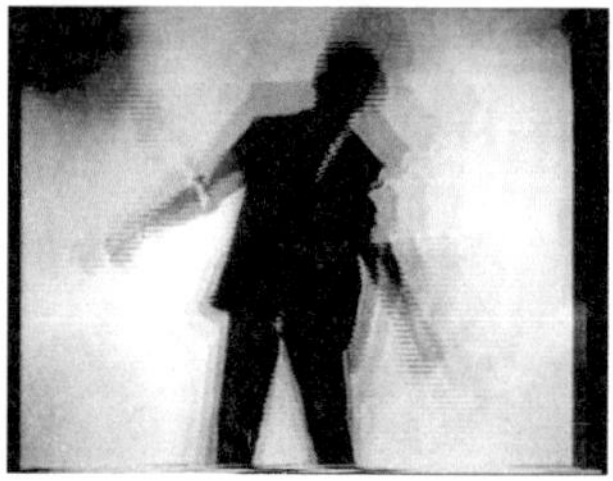

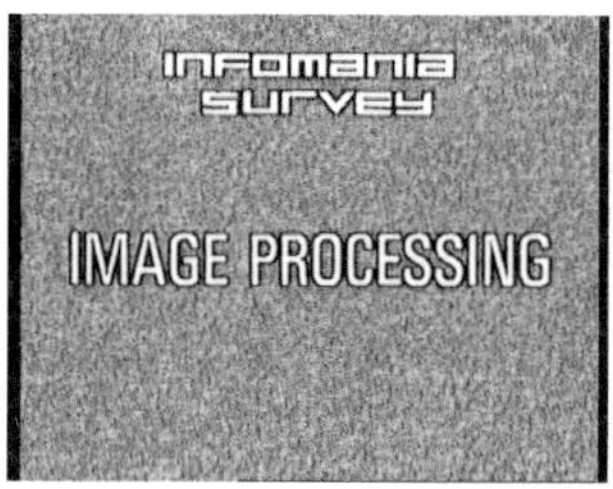

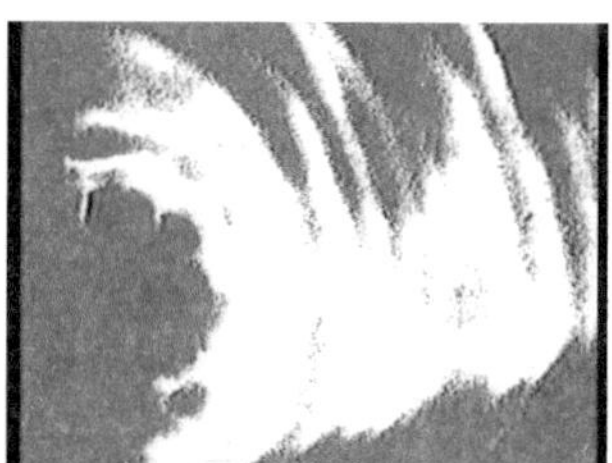

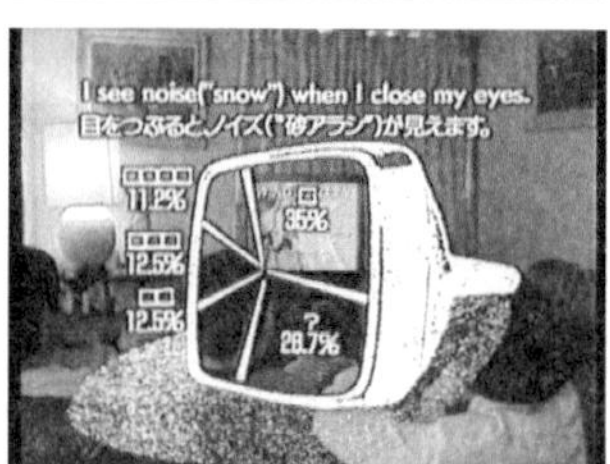

Dan Kidner — But they don't. I've seen the ones that David Curtis has at the Study Collection at Central Saint Martins and they're just plain. There's no label on them.

George Clark — For me this relates to the question of how you show moving images in a gallery: in some way you've got to find a way to understand that work as an object, if we understand the gallery as a place dedicated to the display of objects. What you have are these things that are non-objects or that are non-artefacts, and what do you do with them? In a lot of instances, in a museum for example, they would receive the status of designed object.

Dan Kidner — But that's a product of a certain contemporary exhibition convention, isn't it? Because archives, when presented in art galleries, become art objects. Or rather, I guess they're required to do two things at once: they are required to be artworks or surrogate artworks, but also to actually represent history in a direct way.

James Richards — The posters do at least betray the authored nature of each issue. The issues were singular things. Each editorial team designed its own poster, each edition forged a different identity.

Dan Kidner — In order to take the form of a magazine, the editions of *Infermental* had to promote a very particular relationship to films and videos as discrete works — or rather they had to refute this property. Not only was the structure of the project itself propositional in some important way, the content was also required to have this quality.

George Clark

Infermental fluctuates between the idea of a magazine and the encyclopaedia. One is temporary and specific to a certain time, a certain place, and the other is more authoritative, and transcends the context in which it was made. In what way could the works that were included in the editions be understood as ephemera themselves?

Dan Kidner

I suppose this is the problem that ZKM were faced with when they tried to extract and exhibit individual works from the tapes. Some of the artists were perturbed because the tapes that they had submitted might actually differ from what later became finished and definitive work.

George Clark

An important work in relation to this, and instructive in terms of thinking about how *Infermental* operated as both a record of its time and as a generative structure, is the 1987 video *Cross-Cultural Television* …[7]

Dan Kidner

Which we also included in the exhibition, and which constituted an entrance point in terms of thinking about some of these issues.

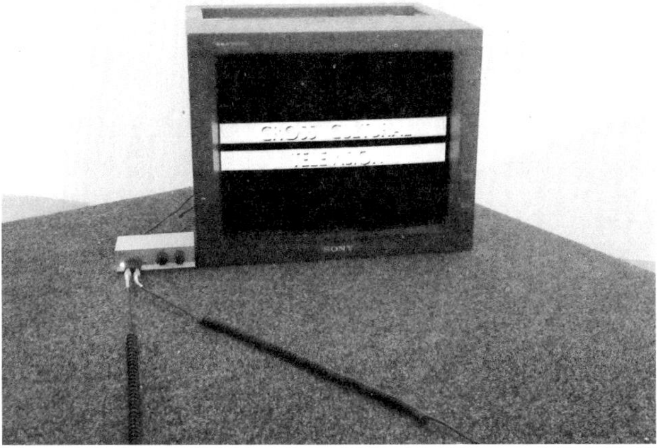

Installation view of 'Infermental',
Focal Point Gallery, Southend-on-Sea, 19 July to 4 September 2010, photo by George Clark.

Cross-Cultural Television, video, colour, Antoni Muntadas and Hank Bull, 1987.

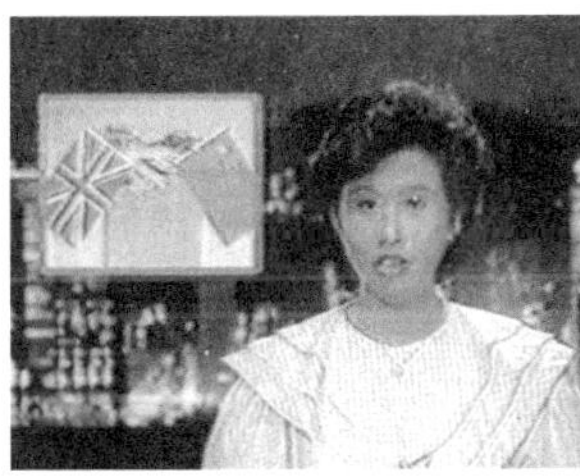

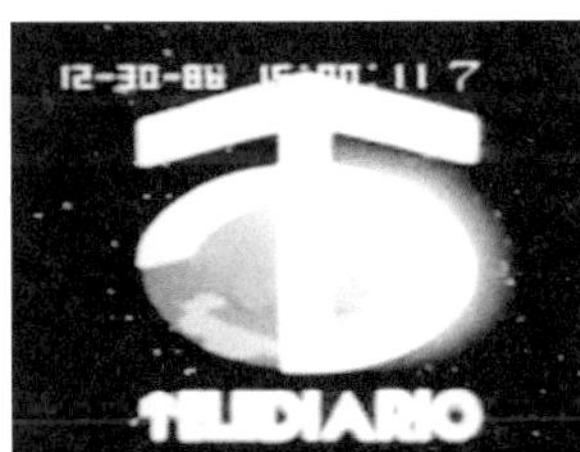

7
'This is a videotape about Television. It is a fragmented, personal view. It is only one of many ways to explore television. This is a videotape about the cosmetics and packaging of television. It is about editing.' Antoni Muntadas. For more about *Cross-Cultural Television* (1987) see www.eai.org/title.htm?id=657

James Richards: For *Cross-Cultural Television*, Hank Bull[8] and Antonio Muntadas[9] invited people to submit video recordings from their local television networks, and from the tapes they made this amazing compilation work, that categorised information: idents and channel logos; channel intros; the presentational styles of news readers. It is a catalogue of the language of television in the 1980s.

George Clark: It is also the only unique project made by *Infermental* — it was distributed with an edition, but also stood apart.

James Richards: When we first talked about how we could present the project, we discussed making a compressed edit of all the graphic elements used in the editions. It would have isolated the voice or language of editorship.

In the end this seemed problematic because of issues over rights but also because of the length.[10] It would have been nice if it could have been a work that would have lasted about five minutes. But it would have probably been closer to an hour, as the idents and graphic segues used in the editions are sometimes quite long.

George Clark: In a way, the inclusion of *Cross-Cultural Television* signalled an interest in the use of idents and graphics in the mid-1980s.

8
For more information about Hank Bull see www.ccca.ca/c/writing/b/bull/bul001t.html

9
For more information about Antoni Muntadas see www.eai.org/artistBio.htm?id=285

10
Rights for each issue are managed by the respective editors. When works were submitted, artists agreed to inclusion in the issue and to share in revenue generated by exhibition or sale of the issues.

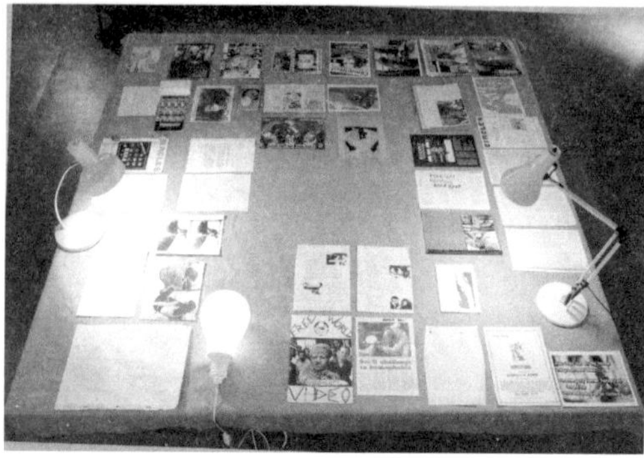

'Reproductive Labor' at The Showroom, 2011.

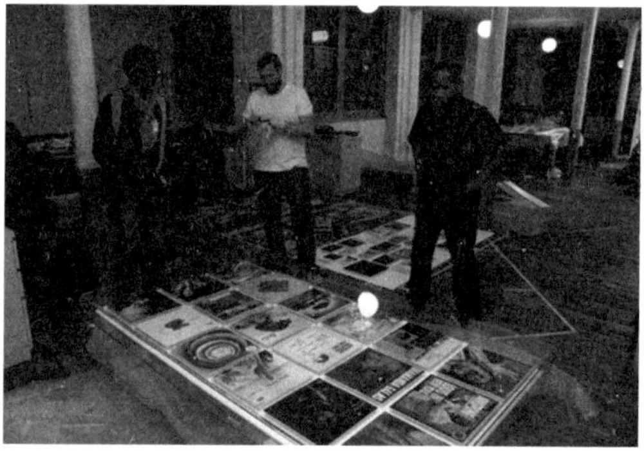

Black Audio Film Collective framing records for display in 'The Ghosts of Song' exhibition, 2007.

11
'Reproductive Labour: An Exhibition Exploring the Work of Cinenova', 9 February to 26 March 2011, The Showroom, London, curated by the Cinenova Working Group.

12
'The Ghosts of Songs: A Retrospective of the Black Audio Film Collective', FACT, Liverpool, 2 February to 1 April 2007, curated by The Otolith Group (Kodwo Eshun and Anjalika Sagar). The catalogue *The Ghosts of Songs: The Art of the Black Audio Film Collective*, eds. Kodwo Eshun and Anjalika Sagar, p.256, 2007, Liverpool University Press, UK.

James Richards

It was possible to compare how the editing and graphic elements of *Infermental* related to those used in mainstream broadcasting.

George Clark

That's also relevant in how we treated the posters for the show. At the time those posters had a very specific function. So by reprinting them and trying to present them in this deliberately estranged manner was to try and throw light on the idea that here was something that was temporary that has become permanent.

Dan Kidner

Just at the level of presentation, what would've been at stake if we hadn't done that? For example, if we had just displayed the original posters? I think it was interesting to try to counter that impulse, and to think about what these exhibitions of film archives — from the recent Cinenova exhibition at The Showroom in London [11] through to the Black Audio Film Collective exhibition curated by The Otolith Group at FACT in 2007 [12] — are actually involved in.

What I find quite interesting about some of these projects is the sense in which at some level they appear to be unmotivated by any concerns other than a desire to present a body of work. But the gallery is not a neutral space, and histories are not static.

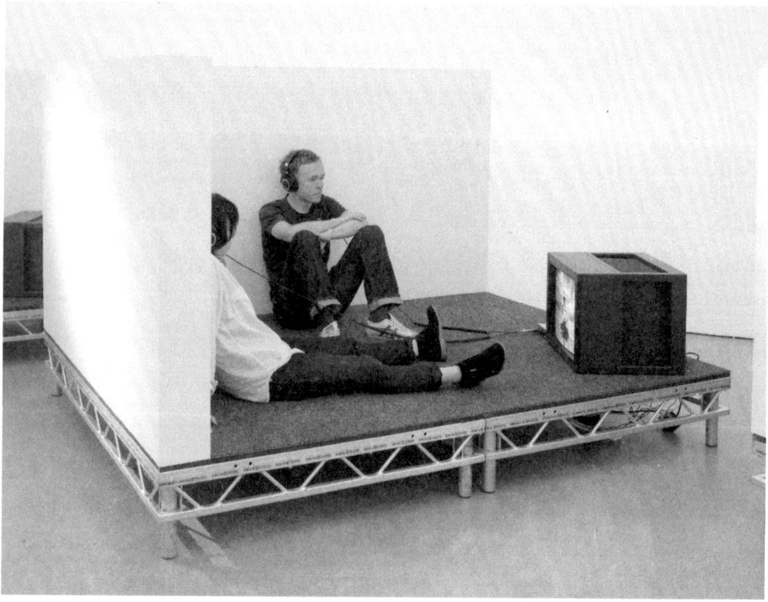

Installation view of 'Infermental', Focal Point Gallery, Southend-on-Sea, 19 July to 4 September 2010, photo by Andy Keate.

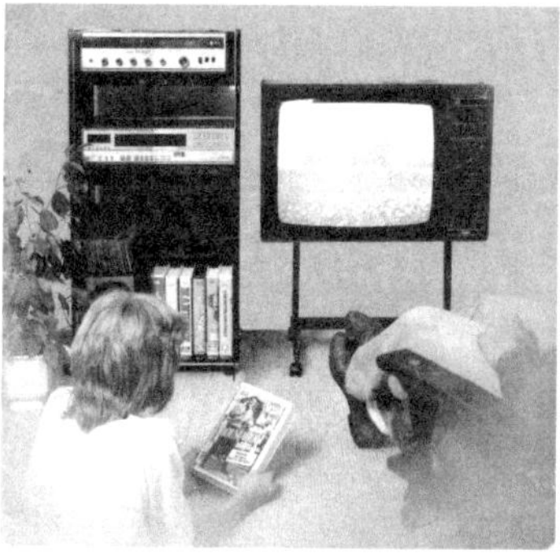

Vintage advertising photo of people watching VHS tapes, c. 1985.

George Clark: Because of the overlap of certain types of display within artistic practice, there's no neutral display anymore …

Dan Kidner: If there ever was …

George Clark: The other question is: what does that mean for the spectator? How do people engage with this type of display, and what type of engagement were we expecting? I think some people found the presentation opaque, in part because it was impossible to sit there and view everything.

Dan Kidner: Though, perversely, this is what the presentation seemed to demand.

James Richards: Well, we were making a place that, hopefully, allowed people to be with it and spend time with it. As much time as possible with the least historical framing.

George Clark: The finish and the smooth surface of the posters was important, as were the surfaces of the viewing booths — all seamless, clean lines. In some ways it was a show about those various surfaces.

James Richards: This austere modular look was important. But also the equipment we used, which referred to the pre-digital age.

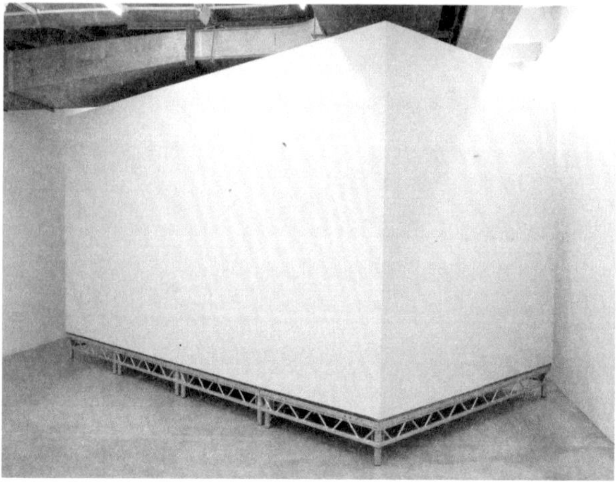

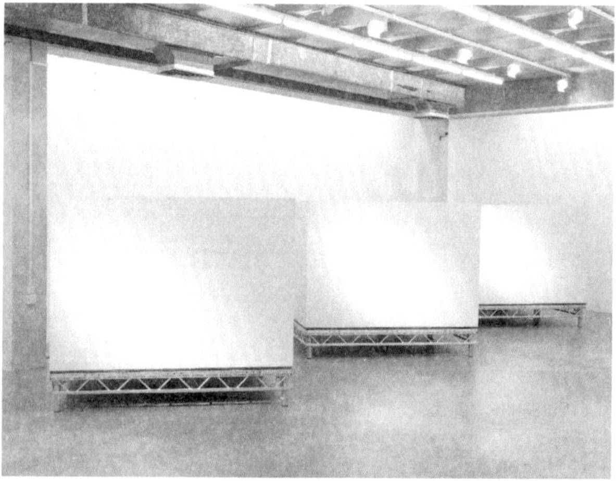

Installation views of 'Infermental', Focal Point Gallery, Southend-on-Sea, 19 July to 4 September 2010, photo by Andy Keate.

13
Active Negative Programme was exhibited as part of two survey shows conceived as 'showcases' for young artists. It was first shown as part of 'Nought to Sixty' at the Institute of Contemporary Arts, London, 4 to 11 August 2008 and then at the show 'The Generational: Younger Than Jesus' at the New Museum, New York, in 4 August to 7 December 2009.

Dan Kidner We used Sony Cube Monitors for the show. Along with Hantarex, these have now become the default monitors for showing video work in the gallery space — particularly video work from the 1970s and 1980s. James, for your 2010 'Art Now' exhibition at Tate Britain you actually fabricated stands to specifically house classic Hantarex cubes. I think you were designing them at the same time that we were working on the booths for the Focal Point Gallery show.

James Richards That's right. With both projects there was a certain play on function: they are completely functional but also highly aestheticised. I mean that they are not plinths in the sense that, through the conventions of the exhibition, one has agreed to ignore plinths. But these structures are very much there and part of the work. The first time I used the Lite-Deck staging was in 2008 in the piece *Active Negative Programme*, where it was used to reference conventional trade displays the type you might find at trade fairs or roadshows.[13] Then for the 'Infermental' show it became something else, because we built these modular units on top of stages.

On a really practical level, it was important that the gallery was very clean and clear because we were showing twenty hours of material, and we didn't want the show to be overwhelming. It was also important to give the visitor space to really concentrate on the material — so these booths were very functional.

For archival shows that include a lot of material, sometimes knowledge of how much there is to see stops you getting really lost in it. There's a limit to how much you can commit to a video, especially when you know that it's a seven-hour compilation. For me it made sense to build something that limited the amount of visual distraction, so it was possible to sit and engage for a long time and not be constantly distracted by another screen or something in the corner of your eye.

George Clark
Often when there is a monitor in a lit gallery show it's hard not to start looking around, at other works on the walls …

James Richards
And at other people. At Focal Point Gallery, because of the way the units were positioned, you weren't aware of people entering the room.

Dan Kidner
One thing that I really became aware of as we were installing was that, if you squinted, it looked like a show from the mid-1960s, perhaps a show of Robert Morris sculptures at the Dwan Gallery circa 1966.[14] As you walked into the gallery the first view of the exhibition was of one big, pale green cube and three smaller ones.[15] These forms were really important because the viewer was never

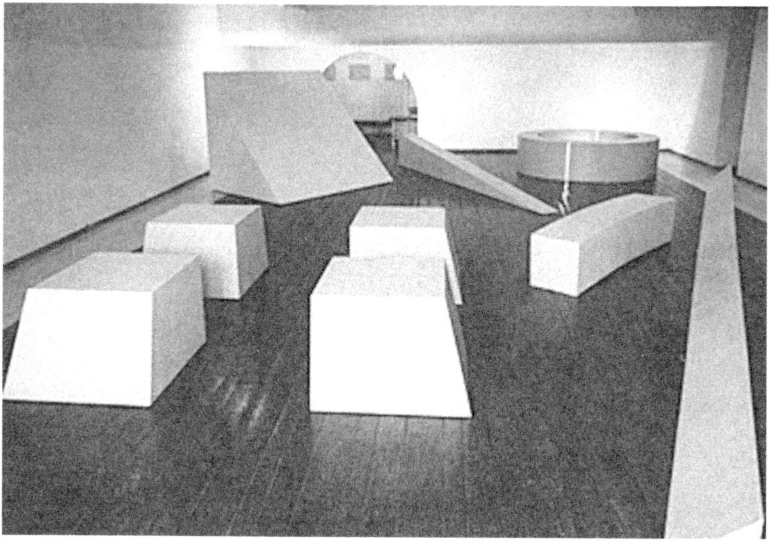

Installation view of 'Robert Morris — One Man Exhibition' at the Dwan Gallery, New York, 1966.

14
Virginia Dwan operated two galleries in Los Angeles (1959 to 1967) and New York (1965 to 1971).

15
The exact shade was Foyer Green from ICI.

Sony Cube 20” monitor, images courtesy The Block.

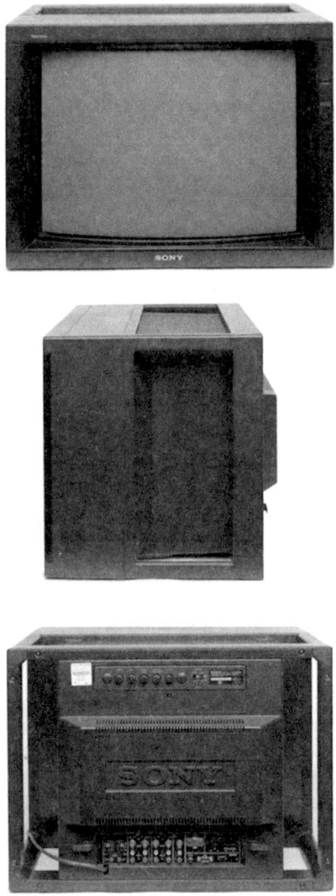

16 Nicolas Bourriaud, *Relational Aesthetics*, (Les Presses du RéeL, France, 1998).

able to escape the fact that he or she was in an exhibition that had been designed in a very particular way — even if it wasn't immediately apparent why it had been designed this way.

There are certain exhibition conventions that come out of the 1960s. Audiences now tend to interpret the meanings of artworks at the level of exhibitions, rather than at the level of individual works. In many ways the issues around presentation that were reflected upon then have been filtered though discussions of performance art, institutional critique, installation art and the 'relational' and participatory practices of the intervening years.[16] Whatever one exhibits now, in a gallery, whether it be films or archives, or whatever, the discourse of exhibitions is hard to ignore. I think reusing these forms, and reflecting on these histories — and on these different discourses — allowed us to signal the different moments in recent exhibition history that moving-image works must negotiate in order to find a space for themselves in the gallery.

When you did actually physically negotiate these structures and sit inside one, on the carpeted platforms, a very different type of space opened up. And a very different understanding of the gallery space, than the more phenomenological understanding associated with that particular strand of North American minimalism from the 1960s.

It was much more domestic in scale, but somehow corporate too, like the floor of a 1980s office — there was always that tension. In that way there was also something of Dan Graham's *New Space for Showing Video* (1995) about the piece.[17]

George Clark — But I think that's the idea, or the proposition. What does that say about *Infermental*'s ambition to create alternative modes of display and engagement with art and its ambition to create a new kind of institution?

Dan Kidner — On one level what we did with the exhibition — or tried to do — is signal the failure of that ambition. In a way, I think we were keen to make clear that the utopian aspect of the project was thwarted.

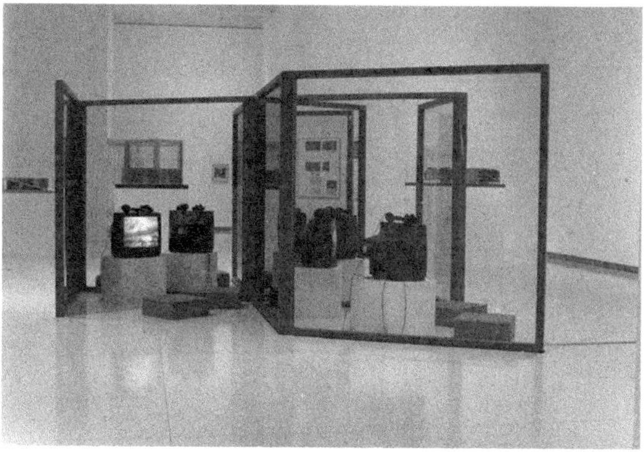

Installation view of 'Dan Graham: Beyond,' Walker Art Center, Minneapolis, 24 October 2009 to 24 January 2010. Pictured: *New Space for Showing Videos* (1995), two-way tempered mirror glass, clear tempered glass, mahogany.

17
Dan Graham's *New Space for Showing Video* (1995) explores the architecture of exhibitions. The work consists of a series of glass panels in mahogany frames that interconnect to form partitioned spaces for monitors showing video works. It was acquired by the Walker Art Center, Minneapolis, USA, in 2002. Graham has also explored issues of video display in many of his published texts, in particular in the book *Video, Architecture, Television: Writings on Video and Video Works, 1970–78* (ed. Benjamin H. D. Buchloh, The Press of the Nova Scotia College of Art and Design, New York University Press, 1979).

A Detour Around Infermental
George Clark, Dan Kidner, James Richards

This publication follows the exhibition 'Infermental' curated by George Clark and Dan Kidner with James Richards, Focal Point Gallery, Southend-on-Sea, 19 July to 4 September 2010.

Edited by George Clark, Dan Kidner and James Richards
Transcription of original recorded material by Robert Cliff
Copy editing by Sam Thorne and Andrew Hunt
Photography of the exhibition at Focal Point Gallery by Andy Keate
Book design by James Langdon
Printing and binding by Cassochrome, Waregem, Belgium
Printed in an edition of 1,000

Published by Focal Point Gallery, Southend-on-Sea, 2012

ISBN 978-1-907185-06-9

Focal Point Gallery
Southend Central Library
Victoria Avenue
Southend-on-Sea
Essex SS2 6EX, UK

southend onsea BOROUGH COUNCIL

Supported by ARTS COUNCIL ENGLAND

Focal Point Gallery

Director: Andrew Hunt
Exhibitions and Marketing Officer: Laura Bowen
Exhibitions and Marketing Officer (Maternity Cover): Lib Fox (January to November 2011)
Curatorial Associate — Offsite Projects: Saim Demircan
Education and Outreach Officer: Fran Wilde
Education and Outreach Officer: Sharon Byrne
Education and Outreach Officer — Offsite Projects: Eve Smith
Technician: Richard Whitby
Exhibitions Interns:
Leila Smith (July to December 2011), Robert Cliff (March to July 2011), Mark Couzens (November 2010 to February 2011), Lib Fox (June to October 2010), Jamie Stevens (January to April 2010).

Acknowledgements: Thomas Beard, Richard Birkett at Artists Space, New York, Anja Casser at Badischer Kunstverein, Karlsruhe, Rebecca Cleman at EAI, Ben Cook and Mike Sperlinger at LUX, David Curtis at The British Artists' Film and Video Study Collection, Claudia Gehrig and Hartmut Jörg at ZKM/ Zentrum für Kunst und Medientechnologie Karlsruhe, Ed Halter, Maren Hobein at Goethe-Institut London, Polly Staple and Jamie Stevens at Chisenhale Gallery, London, Sebestyén Kodolányi at Balázs Béla Stúdió/BBS, Emilie Bujes, and Laurin Federlein.

Special thanks to Vera Baksa-Soós.

We would also like to thank all of the original editors of *Infermental* for their help, and the numerous artists who contributed to *Infermental*.

Infermental editors and contributors:
Vera Baksa-Soós, Alfred Birnbaum, Hank Bull, Gérard Couty, Péter Forgács, Gusztáv Hámos, Astrid Heibach, Mike Hentz, Antonio Muntadas Keiko Sei, and Christian Vanderborght.

George Clark lives and works in London and Los Angeles. His curatorial projects include 'No Wave: New York 1976-1982', Glasgow Film Festival, Worm, Rotterdam; Cinéma Nova, Brussels (2011); 'Infermental' with Dan Kidner and James Richards, Focal Point Gallery, UK (2010) and 'Essentials: Secret Masterpieces of Cinema', Tate Modern and touring (2008). He is a contributing curator to the 6th Bangkok Experimental Film Festival and the curator of the Lav Diaz focus at the AV Festival, Newcastle upon Tyne (both 2012). His writings have been published in *Afterall*, *Art Monthly*, *Mousse Magazine*, *Senses of Cinema* and *Sight & Sound*. He also collaborated with Beatrice Gibson on the script for the film *The Future's Getting Old Like The Rest of Us* (2010).

Dan Kidner is a curator and a writer, and is currently director of Picture This, Bristol. He was previously director of City Projects, London, where he produced the films *Fulll Firearms* by Emily Wardill, *Tenant* by Grace Schwindt (both 2011), *Abyss* by Knut Åsdam and *The Empty Plan* by Anja Kirschner and David Panos (both 2010). Recent curated exhibitions include 'Infermental' with George Clark and James Richards, Focal Point Gallery, UK (2010) and 'Depression' with Lisette Smits, Marres Centre for Contemporary Culture, Maastricht, The Netherlands (2009).

Typographer Will Holder once read that oral tradition would lead us out of the post-modern condition, and has since become preoccupied with 'publishing.' Said publications may not always take the form of ink and paper, and a large part of the preoccupation is spent in finding suitable 'forms' which scrutinise a linguistic means of representation. Holder is editor of *F.R.DAVID*, a journal concerned with reading and writing in the arts (published by de Appel, Amsterdam). In May 2009, he co-curated 'TalkShow' at the ICA — an exhibition/events programme dealing with speech and accountability. He is currently editing (with Alex Waterman) a biography of American composer Robert Ashley, for four or more voices (forthcoming); and rewriting William Morris' *News from Nowhere* (1876) into a serially published guide for design education and practice — set in 2135.

James Langdon is a graphic designer whose practice is concerned with the representation of art and ideas. He has worked in close collaboration with artists such as Céline Condorelli, Matias Faldbakken, Paul Harrison and John Wood, Sofia Hultén, Victor Man, and Joanne Tatham and Tom O'Sullivan and for institutions and publishers including Artangel, London; Book Works, London; Contemporary Art Gallery, Vancouver; Ikon Gallery, Birmingham; Lux, London; Modern Art Oxford; Spike Island, Bristol and Sternberg Press, Berlin. He is one of six founding directors of the artist-run gallery Eastside Projects in Birmingham and is active as a curator, editor and writer.

James Richards is an artist. He was born in Cardiff in 1983 and lives and works in London. Recent solo exhibitions include Chisenhale Gallery, London (2011); Rodeo Gallery, Istanbul (2011); 'DISAMBIGUATION' (in collaboration with Steve Reinke), Trinity Square Video, Toronto (2009) and Swallow Street, London (2009). Recent group exhibitions include 'Clunie Reid and James Richards', Art Now, Tate Britain (2010); 'The Generational: Younger Than Jesus', The New Museum, New York (2009) and 'Nought to Sixty', ICA, London (2008).

Colour pages throughout:
James Richards *Untitled (1–10)*, 2011.